Antony

Says ...

BY THE SAME AUTHOR

NUNSHIGUM, On The Road To Mandalay
  Life in a tank crew in the 14th Army, Assam/Burma 1943-1946

NEMESIS FROM BURMA, The Bamboo Murders

THE PATH
  A story, over the past 5 million years, of our predecessors, and
their journeys of discovery, leading up to the present time.   It
indicates the start of spiritual awareness, the effect of compassion,
and of human nature!

Antony
Says ...

[signature: Arthur F. Freer]

Via

Arthur F. Freer

First published in 2006
by
A F Freer
1 Westbrook Park Close
Woodston
Peterborough
PE2 9JQ

© Arthur F Freer 2006

ISBN 10: 0-9553680-0-6
ISBN 13: 978-0-9553680-0-4

Printed in England by Booksprint

CONTENTS

PREFACE

This experience really started early in 2005, during a quiet evening at home. Conversation had ranged over many subjects, when Carole suddenly said, "Let's see if there is anyone there willing to come and talk to us". She meant, from the other side!

During the past ten years, I have learnt a lot about the spiritual way of life from my wife. She had given me the benefit of her thirty years experience as a clairvoyant and encouraged me to have an open mind when there is any discussion on the subject, so I readily agreed, and we waited patiently.

We sat quietly, with our eyes closed, when I heard a voice that was to become so welcome in our home. "My greetings to you, it is good to have this opportunity to talk with you both!" Carole answered with her blessings and welcome to this visitor. He seemed to be friendly, enough, but declined to give his name, so we settled for calling him, 'The Visitor'.

That first meeting lasted about ninety minutes, with each side asking and answering many questions. It was fascinating. The Visitor told us that he was one of a group of advanced spirits who wished to help us to learn more about the 'life after death'; his answers would only be limited by our own ability to understand them. He gave us some beautiful philosophy and we really regretted not having recorded all his visits.

Over a period of months, he told us that he would like us to form a small group of like-minded friends who could meet regularly in order to improve our knowledge of the spiritual world. ("No pressure", he assured us). At the same time, we asked him to give us his name. He did this, telling us that we would not be able to remember it! It is 'Ywahuntae' and is pronounced with the speaker inhaling his breath on the middle syllable. Needless to say, we did forget it and we still have a problem in pronouncing it. It was his suggestion that we call him Antony, and we readily agreed.

ANTONY SAYS ...

On Tuesday 29th November 2005, we had our first group meeting at home, which was opened with a prayer by Carole, followed by the Lord's Prayer. We had been joined by our friends, Maria and Phyllis, for this meeting with Antony, who had agreed to our using a digital gadget in order to be able to create both CD's and a typed record for a possible book. This is it.

Antony has suggested that he adds a post script of guide lines on how to create your own group for a similar link with spirit. That will be added at the end of this book.

AFF

ANTONY SAYS ...
CHAPTER ONE

It is good to see you, to greet you. The small group is getting bigger. Welcome. I will be pleased to answer questions, one at a time, and, if you have further questions, following my answers, you may ask them. I will ask Carole to control those questions.

C. Did you wish to say any more to introduce yourself to our two sitters?

With pleasure. You call me Antony because my real name is not easily remembered. It had been forgotten many times. The name is 'Ywahuntae', and that is not easy for you, 'Antony' is better.

My purpose, here with you, is on behalf of my group, from what you call a high level in the spirit world. We prefer to call it a 'more advanced level'. It is a matter of words. I am one of this group. I am linked with them, permanently, indefinitely, for all eternity. We have worked together for a very long period, of time that you cannot imagine, in places that you have never heard of and cannot imagine. But the purpose of being with you this evening is to help you, each individual, on your own personal path. You are all well advanced, amongst those on the Earth plane, in your awareness of spiritual truth, and you have an understanding of the nature of progress from healing, unconditional love being sent to others. That is one of the basic facts of which you are completely aware, and you practise it. But, you are on your paths to continue progress. You may have doubts in your minds as to methods, responsibilities, systems, involved. If you have such doubts, or you want to develop your limited knowledge of any one aspect of spiritual progress, this is an opportunity for you to ask a question and for me to give you an answer. Now, back to Carole.

C.   Thank you, Antony.   Would Phyllis like to ask the first question?

P. Good evening, Antony.   I would like to ask, when coming on to the Earth plane, do we ourselves choose which tasks to do, or are we told?

Before a soul is born into a child's body, that soul is a fully independent spirit with the freedom of choice of everything that it will do in the future.   That freedom of choice applies to all and cannot be removed.   So, when a decision is made for a soul to develop in a body, on the Earth plane, the decision to go there comes from that soul, after it has had the opportunity to ask questions from more advanced souls in, what you call, higher levels, more experienced souls, those who have, perhaps, been on the Earth plane many times and made further progress in the spirit world.   That progress will eventually take them, those experienced ones, to a stage of advancement where they do not feel any benefit from further experience on the Earth plane.   So, the advice they give to a developing soul, who has asked them for that advice, that guidance, will be to explain that the purpose of your moving to the Earth plane is for your own personal progress.   You retain freedom of choice.   It is for your own personal progress, so the choice is made by the individual.   The selection of which family, which nation, which part of the world to go to is helped with the advice of those experienced helpers. Does this answer your question?

P.   Thank you, yes.

C.   Maria?

M.   There is much talk in your world, the world of spirit, Antony. When I have asked this question once before, I was told that there was no level, at all, and I cannot understand that.   There are advanced levels.   Do you belong to the white brotherhood of man?

CHAPTER ONE

These questions are to help you on your path, to help you make progress. My origins have been questioned before, and, where it is not of benefit to delve into my origins, there is no answer given. Carole has asked questions similar to that. The question of levels; it is a word which I do not use personally. I have commented before, to Carole, that we refer to 'more advanced awareness', which you call a higher level. I have explained to Carole, before, that spirits of more advanced awareness know their status, they know their point of progress on their own individual path. The more advanced they are, the more they tend to form groups of similar souls, in a similar state of advancement. They tend to work together, to be linked together. And, you mention a name which could apply to a group where you have had contact before, but the name of the group is unimportant. The stage of advancement of that group is of importance. Those of a more advanced stage are able to help those of a less advanced stage. In other words, using your terminology, those of a higher level can help those of a lower level. But, we do not like these words, 'levels'. They tend to be counted. It has been said that there are twelve levels. This is a history lesson for you, for academic reasons. It has been said there are twelve levels. From the lowest to the highest, being the range from complete utter darkness and misery, where the dark elements originate, and from where they travel to try to damage those in the light. If you number these, it is so rigid, that it becomes almost unreal. But, if you imagine each of those twelve levels, having four separate grades within the level, one, two three and four, (grade five would be grade one of the next level), does that help you to picture the stages of advancement? If you go up to the top of level twelve, that is the point of the end of eternity for each soul. The next stage is complete unity with the great white light of spirit, and you could say that there are just two levels there. We cannot imagine them, other than being a great white light of complete, utter, bliss, perfection, joy; the aim of each one of us at this point of your time. Have I given you enough information?

M. Yes, thanks, I can understand that. Thank you.

There are many things, which, if explained to you now, in the terminology of the higher, more advanced levels, as you call them, would not help you to understand. It has been said many times that the total knowledge of facts on the Earth plane is a small part of 1% of all the knowledge available to the more advanced stages, more advanced levels, so there is a lot to learn. And that is our wish, that you will open your mind to learn what you can, talk about it with those who understand, and help them to develop and make progress, because the whole massive purpose of God's will is the reunification of all those sparks of spirit which have gone out as individuals, with individual abilities, wishes, desires, decisions, of which you are one. Each of you in this room is one spark from God. That is why you call God, Father, and he calls you daughter. We call each other brother and sister. Have you a supplementary question?

M. Yes. The other question is why is the teaching, on this Earth, so much about angels?

What teaching are you talking about?

M. The teachers, various spiritual teachers, on the plane, teaching about angels. Is it so that people can understand better, or, why use angels?

The answer to that could be why not use angels?
The picture of angel, being a beautiful looking man, in a night dress, with a pair of wings, is encouraging for children. Children like to feel reassured and safe, and that picture is reassuring for them. But, there are many stories that are told to children to help them to develop their minds, to open their minds to other thoughts, to help them to take those first, hesitant steps on the path forward. It is reassuring for older people to think of angels, who sometimes appear in normal dress and do a good thing. Is

it an angel who helps you meet a stranger, to whom you are attracted, and who is attracted to you? What is it that brings the two together to talk on all subjects, including spiritual progress? It is a reassuring thought, and knowledge, that there are beings thinking about you and wishing you well. But, if there were no angels there would still be souls thinking about you and wishing you well. Do you agree?

M. Yes.

You sound doubtful?

M. To my mind, angels are evolved souls, if that is right?

Angels certainly are advanced souls, and helping you to advance your soul, and you could be an angel! It is all part of the spiritual world. Look at the other side of the coin. There are dark souls who started on the right path and made the wrong decisions, decisions to hurt, to kill, to destroy and to create havoc amongst their fellow beings, when on the Earth plane. Those dark souls are not angels. They are tainted with the darkness of those shadows from the lower regions, the lower areas, the lesser advanced, or the non-advanced levels, as you call them. So there are a variety of so-called spiritual beings, helping, or doing damage, fighting against, or fighting for, and that is the turmoil that you find on the Earth plane, and it has been there for many centuries. Does that help you?

M. Yes. That is fine. That is exactly how I thought it was.

C. I would like to ask a question, please.
We understand that every word and every action is recorded and given to each soul after transition. How are these records kept?

In one word. Impeccably!

ANTONY SAYS ...

You are wondering, by what method are they kept?

A fairly recent invention on the Earth plane is the computer. These wonderful machines, with large abilities to retain a vast amount of knowledge, have become vital in your world today. Those who try to imagine education, the development of the brains of those who design these machines, and who design them for the development of every aspect of human and animal life, amaze many on the Earth plane, they are so advanced. The majority on the Earth look at these machines with awe and are aware of their inability to understand them. But, they can understand how to use them. They are a very recent development in so-called civilised life. But, in each soul, whether a free moving soul, or one within a body, there is a computer, so far advanced, ahead of the machines about which we have been talking, that computer, created by God, has been developed, as man has been developed, within the brain. The human brain is an extremely advanced computer, so far ahead of the machines that it is astounding to all. So, each soul, after being born, with a clear empty mind, has this computer. As it opens its eyes, it records seeing things, its mother, its family, its home, its toys, its pet animals, the early days at school. All that knowledge is poured into that brain and stored; far, far more knowledge than can be contained, if all the computer machines on the Earth were linked together. Far more is retained in the brain of that individual. Every experience, every decision made, every word spoken, every word heard or read, is retained. As the child is educated and grows to maturity it continues to store knowledge, on top of knowledge, and more and more. And, whilst, during that life, in that body, it may have difficulty in recalling what it said, twenty years before, it does retain, and it can recall, the faces of loved ones, the scents and the sounds of nature, the taste of food and drink, but, those that it cannot recall are still there, stored in the cells in that brain. That memory is taken back to the spirit world at the time of transition, so the knowledge, of all the good deeds and the misdeeds of that individual, travels with it back to the spirit world, where it can then replay the tapes. Does that help you?

CHAPTER ONE

C. Yes. It is then, when we get from birth to death, or so-called death, that we see where we have done well, where we have failed, and so forth?

That's right.

C. Yes. It is then, where we have done wrong, or hurt somebody, intentionally, is this when we need forgiveness from that person? Yes?

Yes. And from God.

C. Do we make these decisions on our own, how to get this forgiveness, or do we have someone to help us, and direct us into the right way?

From before that soul enters the child, and grows to adult, and returns to the spirit world, guides and helpers are there, available all the time, twenty four hours a day, in your time. So there is always help available, but it is more a question of guidance and the consideration of different options that are presented. The helpers are not there to tell an individual what to do. The individual makes the choice, having assessed the different possibilities, the pros and cons. If I do this what will happen? If I do that what will happen? They will be given answers to those, but the decision is made by the individual. An awareness, at that time, an awareness of the hurt handed out to others, is brought in front of that individual. They fully understand, they feel the hurt that they have handed out. They are shocked by it. It is a shocking experience, but it is a time of shock. Having returned to the spirit world, they realise, from those shocks, where they have made the wrong decisions. It is more important for them to forgive themselves to begin with, not to make excuses, but to realise the negativity of all those hurts, the tears that they have created, the damage that they have done deliberately. All that is stored in that wonderful computer of the mind, and there are plenty of helpers to show the different options. The decision about what to do is, again, with that soul, not with the helpers. Does that help you?

C. Yes, I understand that. It must be very difficult for people. I have a brother who is an atheist, he believes in nothing, as he says, nothing. So, therefore, in a way, those of us who have awareness of spirit life, spiritual truth, we are more responsible, we are more aware of what we are doing, and the way in which we should act. People that have not got this awareness can deliberately go and hurt somebody and think nothing of it. So, in a way, it is harder for us than it is for them, isn't it?

To start with your first words, your brother, who is an atheist, who does not believe in anything? Let us look at the facts. Human beings are noted for not always telling the truth. He may say to you, I am an atheist, to make you feel small, he thinks, to embarrass you, to make humour of your beliefs, to hurt you, but, I would question his statement at source. He is not mentally retarded. His brain has a similar function to yours, or anyone else's, and, he may say, I am an atheist, just as an excuse for not going to church, for not admitting his belief in God. I would not believe him. So, whether his path is easy, because of his statement, or, because yours is more difficult, because of your statement, I would say, let us not look at whether a path is easier or harder, but look at it from another point of view, is it right, or is it wrong? Are you happier with your knowledge of the truth, and the truths, to which you are being introduced, continually, the proof that you receive time and time again, of the effectiveness of your healing abilities in wishing others to feel better. You know the truth. Your brother does not face the truth. I would feel sorry for him and pleased for you.

C. I do, but he has ridiculed me so many times. Both my brothers did. They class me as a 'do-gooder', but, I do not take any notice of that, but, I have tried, many times, to prove to him that we are not in the grave, we do not die and there is continuous life, but he just does not want to know. I think he fears spiritual matters, he fears death. This is why he won't face up to listening to anything concerned with spirit. I have tried. Perhaps, I have succeeded a little, but he will not speak of it. He will not go into anything. We have given much healing to him when he has needed it. I think, really, he is aware of that, because he got better so quickly. So I am hoping that, a little of what has been given to him, he has thought about, for his own sake.

You have recently had proof of his awareness, to some degree, of spiritual matters; when you visited him, he was caressing a beautiful dog, a lovely creature, which you admired, and he, with his arm around it, said, I feel very privileged to be allowed to own this dog. Now, that was a spiritual statement! So, have no fears for him. He is not an atheist. His eyes will be opened more, when he sees the love of that dog for him, and he his love for that creature. You have no need to have anxieties. He has his limitations, and, when he returns to spirit, he will have a period, similar to his brother, a period of shock, facing up to all the unkindness that he has handed out, not only to you, but to many others. That is his problem, his future, his worry, when he has to face it. And you have helped him, a little, to the limit of his willingness to accept, not your willingness to give help. Do you understand that?

C. Yes, he is very much for the material things in life, which is very apparent on the Earth plane today. This is why there is so much, with the young people of today, with the drugs, drinking, and violence. The world is a dark place at the moment, and I just feel that the spiritual truth, the messages, are not getting through to the younger generation, I'm not saying all, but a lot. There is much concern for the parents with their children. Is this because of the darker side of spirit, that they are able to get to these children, when they are on these drugs? Is it because they are more open and the dark elements can get to them better, to influence their minds?

The darkness of which you speak has been on the Earth plane for a very, very, long time, from the early days of mankind. There were those who made the wrong decisions, bad decisions, and they developed chemicals, which have varied over the centuries and thousands of years, all for the purpose of creating apparent, temporary, joy, but, in reality, long lasting misery. There is nothing new in that. The nature of the chemicals changes a little, as some souls find they can create a different effect, with a different reaction, but there is nothing new in the darkness which is spreading. But, the darkness is being beaten. It may take a lot more time, but the only thing that can rule, in the end, is the light. It depends on people like you, Maria and Phyllis, and Arthur, talking about progress, talking about opportunities to get further along the right path. And that is the purpose of my visit.

C. We thank you for that, too.

M. I would like to know, you said, a child will be born with a clear, an empty mind. When, actually does spirit enter this little child, that is created, does spirit enter at that moment of creation or is it at a later point?

The creation of a child, an embryo, from two cells, is the start, and there comes a time when there are sufficient cells created, linked together, functioning according to a programme, which is built within them. That programme contains certain abilities, awareness, but not knowledge, from the father and the mother. Eventually, there is a little independent movement within that embryo, within the mother's womb. It is at about that time that the spirit enters. If that embryo is removed, that is a termination of that life, which had only just started. If it is not terminated, and continues to grow, the only memories retained

CHAPTER ONE

in that wonderful computer of the brain, are the memories of the warmth and the feeling of well-being in that beautifully designed environment, until the first major shock of coming into open air, the birth. That brain is recording that. That is the beginning of its memory. From then on, it develops in the way that I described to you earlier. Does that answer your question?

M. When we talk of termination, the time limit, two months, three months, the embryo, the spirit has entered at this time?

After conception? Up to the time of the quickening? It is during that period that the soul enters the embryo, nearer the quickening rather than the early stages. Time is different in the spirit world. This is a point that I have tried to make before, and I wish to make again. Your timing is made in seconds, minutes, hours, days and weeks, strictly measured, strictly recorded, but, spiritual time is a different dimension. It is moving ahead and behind, simultaneously. We are aware of things in the spirit world before they actually happen, or appear to happen, or are recorded as having happened on the Earth plane. The difference between the two times is something that I cannot explain to you so that you understand it fully, but, please accept that there is a difference in time. They are similar, they are linked, but they are not rigidly locked into one another. So the timing of a spirit entering an embryo may seem terribly important, if you are looking at it from the Earth time, but, looking at it from spiritual time, it is something that happens. The measurement of the split second, in which it happened, becomes unimportant when those two times are linked together, but not rigidly locked together. I don't think that I can explain it much more than that. You can worry too much about when an embryo becomes a living soul. It becomes a living soul when the soul becomes alive within it. Before that it is a potential soul in a living embryo, and the timing of that varies. It is not rigid, so I cannot spell it out to you in that way. There are many minor, (not problems), minor misunderstandings, caused by these two differences in timing.

It is just the same as talking about different levels in the spirit world and different grades of awareness. The only importance between two different grades of awareness, is that those on the higher grade are able to help those on the lower grade, but not in reverse. Those on the higher grade have been there before. They have worked up from it. They have that full knowledge and awareness that is being sought at the lower grade. Have you any further questions?

P. Antony, I would like to ask something, please.

I had a pregnancy of two and a half months. When we go to church, sometimes they say that I had a little daughter that grew up in the spirit world. I can't understand what you have just said, and the connection with what they say in the church.

If you have been advised that you have a baby daughter that has grown up, why would you doubt that? Are you still trying to link the pregnancy in with the spiritual time and the earthly time?

P. I expect so, yes.

I think that that may be causing the difficulty. By all means, take great joy in the knowledge that you will meet that daughter, and you will be delighted with her progress and her awareness, and you will have all the joys of reunification. You would not have been told that, if that daughter had never existed, so, why doubt it?

P. I have not doubted it. I just did not understand.

Do you mean that you like to think that the soul entered your daughter at conception, rather than later?

P. I really don't know, Antony, I can't say yes or no.

CHAPTER ONE

Take the positive joy of having been advised, linked with that daughter through a medium.

P.   Yes, I did.

Continue with that joy!   The linkage can grow stronger, can grow weaker, on any one occasion, but, have every faith in that.

P.   I will.   Thank you.

Have we answered all the questions?

C.   At the moment, until we can find some hard ones.

You have found plenty of hard ones this evening.   I understand the puzzlement caused by these different natures of time.   It is so rigid, on the Earth plane.   And what is time in the spirit world, where we have eternity?   Is it so important?

C.   We say we have to go to bed, go to sleep, and wake up, and, then do all our jobs.   You don't have to go to sleep, do you?

I have forgotten what sleep was!   I see you in your dreams.   I see you when you are asleep, and you are busy working!   So how can you be resting when you are out working?

*C.   That is why we are tired when we wake up, you see.
   Do you remember me asking you, when you first came through Arthur, that I thought you were very severe?   I asked you, doesn't anyone laugh in the world of spirit?   Do you remember?*

And then you told me a joke and made me laugh.

C.   Yes.   Well, we live in troublesome times, so I am sure you are aware, and so, we have to lift ourselves somehow, you understand?

You may have reasons for being downhearted, but, I reassure you, the light will win! It is winning, and you can help it. If you discuss these thoughts, these abilities to link, (which is another experiment). We had an earlier experiment, writing a book, and those who wrote it were delighted with the result.

C. Yes. While you talk about that, how did that actually come about? And, why?

(Pause). I am trying to time it, in your time.
Arthur was late in coming into this movement, or, becoming more aware of this movement. He had been on the fringe, waiting for stimulus, and we had linked with him. One of our group gave him a name, which he used in the book, but, he was advised by a medium that he should write a book. That medium recognised the ability, knowing that he had previously written a book or two, and that he could be used by spirit guides to take dictation. And so, he merely typed the book.

C. That's true.

He typed it at his best speed, and printed it, and sent it for publishing. It was a book, designed not to tell the literal history of the world, exactly dated in your time, but to describe the way humankind had developed, from being smaller, with a smaller brain, living a crude animal life, but with the potential for development. It describes that development, how the brains grew with improved nourishment, improved diet; how, in the early days it was basically a very difficult existence with a short brutal life. Now, people live more than twice what they did in the early days. Remember, in the early days the first ten years, if the creatures lived that long, was a hard learning time of education. Having reached thirty or forty years, with a developed body and a mature mind, much more can be learned. In every year, much, much, more can be learned, in that year, than in the early years. So, it was in the interests of progress that mankind should be able to live longer. But, even then, they tried to stop it, with their fighting, killing. Diseases came along, but they had an ample supply of herbal remedies, and the knowledge, which they acquired and applied, and improving their lot, they faced changes in their methods of communication. Language developed and the mental communication was retarded. There are some now with the ability to send and receive mental messages, but language has detracted from that progress. Then, they became more warlike, developed new and more dangerous weapons, and so it goes on. And that is how the book, the story, came to be told. It is intended to be helpful, educational, interesting, and to encourage people to open their minds to spiritual thoughts, to the receiving of spiritual messages from those of us here, who are trying to communicate. Does that answer your question?

C. Yes. Thank you. We have had very good reports on the book. Some people liked it very much, others found it a bit hard going, as we say, but, the majority of people found it very interesting, so, I feel that it has done good. I think it all depends on the person, if they are willing, as you say, to open their minds and see the bigger picture.

You can imagine how many computerised brains went through the experiences described in the book, and yet it is only a few hundred pages. It is very compact, trying to give an indication of the pressures on people, particularly the urge to move, to travel, to explore. And that was how the Earth's surface was covered with human beings. But now, we sadly see means being used, developing, growing, to eliminate a large percentage of the population, who are creating so much pollution that the nature of the Earth's surface can change during the next hundred years.

C. Yes, we notice it with our own weather, the seasons are not as they used to be.

There always have been changes in the weather. Cold spells, ice ages, warm spells, that has always been the nature of this planet, and will continue. The temperature change is part of nature, it is part of the way of things, and will continue.

C. We understand that it is because of the pollution, the melting of the ice caps.

That is having an affect on it. It has happened before, many times.

C. Right. We do thank you for coming, Antony, and we look forward to meeting you again.

I thank you ladies for joining me. I have enjoyed it. I hope you will bear in mind what you have heard, think about it, question it, think of more questions to bring again, and, pass on the good news. The Light will win. Bless you all.

My greetings to you all.   It is good to be with you.   God bless you all.

I would like to say a few words before you raise your first questions.   The whole purpose of these group meetings is to help each member, in their own advancement, on their own path, leading to greater awareness in the future.   I was aware, at the last meeting, that I was asked two questions, one from each of the two ladies, which I did not answer in the way that the question was formed.   Maria asked me if I was a member of the White Brotherhood.   Now, that question, formed in that way, can be answered in two ways; Yes, or No.   If I had given her either of those answers, it would not have been the full truthful answer to her question, and I will explain why.   I talked around the subject, to a degree, but probably not enough to satisfy a lingering doubt as to why I did not answer more fully.   I had told you all that I was one of a group from an advanced condition, an advanced vibration, or, as you call them, level of spiritual advancement; and, being one of that group, I am permanently linked with that group, as I am now linked with you in this room.

I can tell you that, during the millions of years, when the development of spiritual souls led into a separate entirety, a separate life from the Creator, but still linked with the Creator; as progress was made, groups, of similar stages of advancement, tended to work together.   Two or more souls, working together, have more power than the sum of the power of each individual soul; so you see the benefit, to all concerned, in forming groups? These groups are not of the nature of human groups, where there are rules issued from those forming the group, and membership depends on either an invitation to join, or the payment of a subscription, over a period of time, to become a member.   No, the spiritual groups are a loose linkage of souls, working forward, for self development and for group development, which, as you know, helps other souls who need help. It depends on giving that unconditional help and love to those, with whom they come in contact, who require help, and who are, themselves, advanced by that help.

So these groups, who were, sometimes, asked what their name was, when linking with the human plane, were given a name, usually including the word 'white', to indicate goodness of spirit. A nice name, like white brotherhood, white rose, white daphne, white dahlia; these, and hundreds of other names, have been used by different groups. To be in the membership of one group, has meaning for the soul on the Earth plane, who is in contact, linkage, with that group. And it is reassuring to hear the name, with a feeling of confidence, knowledge; mutual experience confirms the name in the power and goodness of that group, as with the 'white brotherhood', and all the others.

These groups were formed at what you would call levels four, five and upwards. Those of a similar stage of advancement, those groups, working for their own advancement, frequently were working with other similar groups, at a similar stage. They became linked, a spiritual linking.

A. The tape, named Antony Two, stopped after a period of twelve minutes, due to lack of space, and I will now try to recall the other points raised on the Tuesday evening group meeting.

Referring to Maria's question, the groups, which had been formed, and grown in strength, by individuals working together and increasing their power, continued to make progress, and, in time, became linked with other groups of a similar level of advancement. This linkage enabled each member to feel that they were a member of other groups, and so you will see why it was easy to answer Maria's question with both Yes and No. Perhaps that will remove the disappointment.

The other question, which had been asked by Phyllis, regarded the time at which the spirit entered the embryo of a child. She was asked if she could go back, in her memory, to those times, and even to a point before her conception. At that time, she, with guidance, had made the decision who were to be her parents, and so she was aware of the environment in which she would be born. She could imagine that, when her parents conceived, and the tiny embryo started to grow, she would then be interested in every stage. She would visit. She would be moving in and out of that growing foetus, fascinated with the prospect of it becoming her body, and, I think she will agree, that she could not resist entering on a number of occasions, up to the point where it was ready to receive her soul, as a completion of the creation of a new child. So, I could ask her the question, when did her soul enter the embryo? Was it at the time of conception, or was it at any other time between then and the quickening? I think she will agree that it could have been frequently between those points in time? But, when she settled into the growing foetus, in order to remain there and stay in that body, as she is now, her memory of previous life would be wiped clean, and she would then be at the start of this present life, and, I think she agreed that she could understand why she had not been given a short answer to her original question. I hope that this record will be helpful.

ANTONY SAYS ...
CHAPTER THREE

It is good to be with you again. My greetings to you.

C. Good evening, Antony.

Good evening. A smaller group?

C. Yes, but only for this week. We should have Maria back next week.
    We thought that we should start tonight to get us into the New Year. We have lots of questions, quite hard ones! I have a question here about spiritual law. What are these laws, and are there any penalties for abusing these laws? Or, should we say, reprimands?

You put it in the plural, Laws?
    You are moving into the field of long words. There is only really one law, which cannot be ignored, cannot be broken, and must be kept. That is the omnipotence of God. That tells you everything. The overwhelming power of the Creator of all the universes, all the planets, all the creatures on those occupied, the development of each individual creature, the advancement of all types of creature, empowered by the Creator, given capabilities of advancement, bringing us to another law, a subsidiary one, which also cannot be broken; the freedom of each individual to make their own progress, their own decisions. And, with that, accepting the responsibility of their action and how it will affect others concerned.
    If you regard those two as the Law of the Creator, you have sufficient fact upon which to work. On the Earth plane you have a variety of people who create law, and who try to apply it, or several of them try to apply it, but some of them ignore it. They ignore their own law. But you are used to hearing of laws to do

this, do that, not do this, not do that, and there is some cynicism, humour, disbelief, refusal to obey laws; and then the lawmakers do not know how to handle the situation, where their wishes, or their stated wishes, are flouted. That is all part of the suffering torment on the Earth plane. You appoint these people, you give them power, which they abuse, and which you ignore.

So, there is created a testing field for individuals, even just with the law of their own country, their own land. They make decisions to obey, or to disobey. In exactly the same way, they make their own decisions about the law of the Creator. So, in answer to your question, if you wish to know the spiritual law on any point, on any problem which faces you, you can immediately hear the different possibilities. You listen to that inner voice, your conscience; you know the difference between right and wrong. In that situation, why would you want to know or hear of any other laws laid down? You ask about penalties for breaking laws, even the two laws that I mentioned earlier. You know the answer to that. You have heard it before. Every one of your actions, all your activities, thoughts, words, deeds, are recorded, and you know that the day will dawn when you hear the list of occasions when you did not strictly apply the law. So, that answers that question?

C.   So, in that way, you are not answerable to anybody?

Me, or my group?

C.   Yes.   Both.

I, and the other members of my group, have moved through all the varying stages of advancement, to be where we are at this point in your time, and in our time. We have moved through all those stages. We have experienced the imperfections available at every stage; at your stage, at lower levels, as you call them, and at higher levels; imperfections which upset the person or the soul involved, and others, and depending upon the effect on others, within their field of influence; so, the sorrow, the punishment, you might call it, is applied, applied, in my case, by me, until I have received forgiveness for the error, forgiveness from those who have been hurt. So, there is punishment, there is sorrow, there is regret; and there is a stronger desire not to make the same mistake. Over the aeons of time, one moves forward, one learns more, and one learns to avoid making past errors another time, and that is progress. One learns more about the structure of the spiritual world as well as the physical worlds. Have I told you enough?

C. Yes. I just want to pick up on one thing. I don't know if Phyllis wants to ask any questions.

Imperfections, now, we are all imperfect beings, or we would not be on the Earth plane, would we? We are trying to learn and grow spiritually through our errors. We must make mistakes, to grow spiritually, to learn. It is the learning plane. This is where we feel the pain and the suffering. There are many times, as you pointed out, when we make the same mistake over again, until we realise what we are doing. They are hard lessons to learn. The reason I asked that was because we are on a lower level, whilst you are on a higher level, because you have advanced so much and learnt so much. I feel so very inadequate asking these questions, but, on the level of my own understanding, these are the sort of questions that people ask, they want to know, you understand, and it has to be put to them that they are responsible for their own actions. They look for cause and effect. Do you understand why I ask that question? I know, with my own life I have hurt people. They have hurt me. This is how we live here on the Earth plane today; and it is only now I have got older that I have matured more and found understanding. It is only through a lot of heart ache that you find this understanding, and yet I have not found peace of mind.

Let me answer a few of the points before they slip away. You talk about imperfections. That is another way of saying 'lack of perfection'.

CHAPTER THREE

Perfection is the ultimate aim, the goal for all of us, so, imperfections indicate the need to learn, as you say. If you keep making the same mistake and having the same problems, the same disappointments, and you look back and examine the past, you learn from experience, that is a normal process of learning. It starts at school, with the repetition of figures, spelling, and so on. It continues through life. We make the same mistakes, but we realise it when we have the same reaction, the same uncomfortable feelings after doing something, and, looking back, sooner or later, we ask ourselves, why is this happening? The repetition of pain from the same cause gives a repetition of realisation of 'wrongness', and so, sooner or later, the brain develops to the point where the individual asks of himself, or herself, why is this happening, and then they get the answer. The inner voice, the conscience, tells them; I have hurt this person before, or, I have hurt similar persons before, and I have had the same, or similar, results. And, as you say, 'the penny drops'. The realisation comes, and with it the decision to avoid similar situations in the future, and so you avoid similar reactions in the future, and that is another step forward on your path. If you are aware of a lack of peace of mind now, in changing situations, ask yourself, within yourself, where have I gone wrong, what have I done, to be still in a stage of suffering, after a certain action or actions? You have mentioned hurting other people. Ask yourself, have I used an unkind word about someone else again? Is this the sort of thing? And the answer to the problem lies within that area, asking yourself for an explanation, rather than asking me. If I tell you the answer to your question, you may or may not accept that, but, when you hear the answer from within yourself, what can you do but accept it, and learn from it, and make progress immediately afterwards? Does that help you?

C. *Yes, but it is a very hard thing to do.*

Of course it is. It is a hard life. As you say, the Earth plane is an area of hard facts, unpleasant situations, there are unpleasant people.   You read about them in your newspapers and in your news reports, unpleasant happenings, they make the news, you hear of them.   But, fortunately, you do not always experience those same unpleasant things, but you are aware of them.   You are aware of the fallibility of human nature in dealing with others.   There are many, many in your land, who are appalling in their activities, and those same creatures deserve almost pity, if they were not so cruel.   The true love, the unconditional love of spirit, gives them pity, but that does not help them immediately. The difficulty is helping those evil ones to understand that there is a much better alternative to their way of life, to see good in others, not an opportunity for stealing or aggression of any sort. There have been times in past wars, where so much evil has been done by one side, that the other side felt uplifted by their own righteousness.   They felt that they were fighting a war for God, with God on their side; but, that was not the case, because, within their own ranks there were many similar, evil ones, similar to those that they hated and attacked on the other side.   Where are we going to, now?

P.   You have described an observation of mine.   It seems that the older we get, the world is getting more cruel.   There are so many cruelties, murders and robberies, terrible things that happen to human beings.   As you get on, you just cannot believe that people are doing these things to one another.

You have virtually repeated what I have just said.   People can believe it, because it is a fact.   People will have to believe it.   The facts are being told to you, day and night, every day. There has certainly been a great increase in the distribution of so-called news, with the television and the newspapers, whereas, in years gone past, the news was spread by word of mouth, and it took longer, and there was exaggeration. But today there is instant communication, or almost instant communication, and so the awareness is with you for more time each day.   Probably, the easiest way of dealing with it is to send out healing thoughts, as you do, sending them, not only to the victims, but to the perpetrators, for what they have done and what they are going to continue doing, until they change their ways. Sometimes, there are opportunities to speak, in front of others, in an official capacity, to make an official complaint, to increase an awareness of your own dissatisfaction of the trends, the state of the situation, verbally, and in writing to your leaders, to shame them into more decisive action. I understand that you frequently get promises from your politicians; you laugh, I weep. It continues to create a situation on the Earth, a situation of suffering, frustration, pain, stress, which helps to create further illness, the snowball effect. The more voices that are heard, condemning the wrongness, the evil, the more prayers that are said for the protection of yourself and your loved ones, and your property, your loved buildings, your churches. The more prayers that go out, the more help will be received. Have you any more questions?

P.   I have an observation, Antony.   I have written down, here, that, when I go to healing, to be a channel for the healing, people have told me that my eyes become very oriental, and I also feel the difference in my eyes, whilst being with the person.   It is very nice to feel that people come to us, while we are here.   I just wished to say that.

That is a good observation. I will make one. You will have to ask Carole to introduce you to Hsu Lin, who similarly has Asiatic eyes, at this point in his career. It is sometimes wishful thinking, on the part of awakened souls, to see the American Indian, the Chinaman, and so on, their features on the face of a healer, or a speaker, or a medium giving messages from such a spirit, but, it also happens. And, isn't it a joy to feel that your guide, your helper, has been recognised on the features on your face? You will have to tell me if Arthur's features appear similar to mine. Carole tells me that we do not smile very often, but it is good to have a little teasing.

ANTONY SAYS ...

Yes, it is good to be told what you have been told. You have an oriental person working through you, at times, and so that is likely. Bless you.

C. I think that it is my turn again, now.
Could you tell me, Antony, where did the Creator come from?

We are having a humorous evening. Let me tell you some facts of life.

The Creator did not come from anywhere. The Creator is. Full stop. He always has been. He always will be. Whether we call him a 'he' or a 'she' an 'it' or a 'thing', he will always be. He is. There never was a time without. So, he came from eternity. He is eternity. Does that answer your question?

C. What is eternity?

That is another question.

It is for ever. It is everlasting. It is without beginning or end. It is an endless circle that always was, always is, and always will be. And that is telling you, within the limitations of this language.

C. We often refer to it, in spiritualism, as the greater intelligence, the supreme intelligence, a being, a force, a life force. Many people, in other religions, talk about God as a man, that Jesus Christ is the son of God, in his image. To me, when you speak of the Creator, I find it very hard to understand and absorb this great mind, of how it all began in the beginning. Where did this energy, this life force, come from?

We are restricted now by the limitations of the language which you all speak, and use for thought and communication, and, in that language there is no perfect explanation in all our minds, including mine, to explain the answer to your question. We can only accept the information received from the Creator that he is, and always was, and always will be. That is the limitation of language, not the limitation of God. He is unlimited, completely unlimited. One of the points that we have discussed about the different areas, different levels of advancement, is that each movement, forwards and upwards, accompanies a greater awareness and understanding of the facts, the facts of life, totally. As you move forward and advance, you will learn new philosophies, new theories, and new methods of description. You will become more aware of the nature of the light of spirit. My group has become very much more aware than your group, as you know, and we are still advancing. Our desire, our aim, and our purpose, is to learn more and be sufficient to enjoy that complete bliss, about which we have spoken, the complete and perfect reunification with the light of spirit. Now, we are not there yet, but we are very much nearer to it than you are and when I say to you that we do not have the complete and full understanding of it, yet, it is imminent. It may take a few thousand or a few million years, but it is imminent.

Please be assured that we know it is totally right, totally truthful, and indescribably joyful, and our group is moving towards it, as yours will. If you take a step forward, you are a step nearer. If you move up one level, as you call them, you are one level nearer, with opportunities opening up in front of you, new awareness that does not need explanation now; and you will be able to help others, less advanced than yourselves. That is all part of God's plan, all part of the universal truth. So, be joyful, be aware that your trials and tribulations may be unpleasant, at times, in order to make a point to help you increase your awareness of the future and into the future. You speak of other religions, and of God, and of Jesus Christ. The words you use are the words of earlier stages. You call God, He, Him, Father, as though he was masculine. Those are merely comfortable ways of talking about a superior being, using old terminology, and old philosophies. There are those who read of Jesus Christ and laugh. They scorn the thought of a person being born into this world, this world of trial, in which you are, and being perfect and remaining perfect. You could call that another experiment of God.

But, look at the impact that his arrival had on the Earth, and the subsequent result! Even disbelievers date their year from the date of his birth, or the approximate year of his birth. They accept that. They are not fighting to change the number of the year to comply with their own very limited theories. You talk of religions. We say there are no religions in heaven. They are merely limitations of thought of those tied and linked to the Earth plane.

So, those who mock Christianity, or Islam, or Buddhism, they do so for negative reasons. They do not wish to understand the movement towards purity in each of those philosophies and others. It has been said, that if there was no God, the human race would have invented him; and the cynics say, that is what happened, we do not believe in him. You can imagine the situation in which those cynics find themselves, when their words and thoughts are read back to them on their return home? Have I gone on too long?

C. No. No. No. We are brainwashed, here, on the Earth plane, from childhood.

Agreed.

C. And there is so much conflict, caused through religion.

It has been used as an excuse for waging war. Read Arthur's book. It is all in there.

P. Antony. Before we come on to the Earth plane, are we in groups ourselves? Not in understanding as high as you are now, but could you please explain this question. Are we in little groups, at all?

I am glad that you asked that question. You are thinking constructively on spiritual lines, showing a desire to learn and advance your own knowledge, and make progress. That is good.

CHAPTER THREE

Before you come to this Earth, you are still in heaven, a spirit. You have certain abilities, God-given abilities, to be able to travel anywhere, wherever you wish, instantly. You have the ability to overhear conversations, on the Earth plane or elsewhere. You can develop in the spirit world and make progress. There are opportunities to learn. You have heard of the Halls of Learning? They are not a university college, as you understand it. They have a similar affect, but they are all-embracing, on different levels, linked or not linked. The opportunities for learning are there and progress is made. But, Carole will ask this question, where did those souls come from? And that is where I mention again about the sparks of spiritual goodness, the sparks from God. A tiny light, in your mind, is a spirit with a clear conscience, a clear mind, but with that little, wonderful, computer, built in, starting to learn, mixing with other spirits of more experience, as you are doing now, learning, remembering, applying the knowledge that you learn in that way, to every experience in front of you. And, then you become aware of other spirits, operating within bodies on the Earth plane. You see them with their body, growing from a little child to an adult and then returning home, for some reason or other, the main reason being that they have taken their transition, for whatever reason.

In those years, as you know, they are learning from their experience here, a harder, a physical, life. But, it is a life which has new blessings, the blessings of companionship, the two sexes enjoying life, enjoying each other, giving, receiving and creating offspring to bring another new life into the world, and so on. You are fully aware of that side of it? There is a lot of joy, a lot of bliss; and a lot of untruth and darkness. Those still in the spirit world are aware of this, and they acquire, not only an ability to overhear conversations, and to join in some of the experiences; but they become able to link with the minds of those on the Earth plane. All those on the Earth plane have the latent ability to become aware of the spiritual souls wishing to contact them. They have thoughts. They see pictures. They smell smells. They taste things. It is strange. They are aware of something happening. They think, is it a voice of conscience? And so, over the ages, as mankind developed, as the brain developed, these abilities grew to the point where contact was made. That contact can be made in a multitude of ways.

One can be walking in the country and suddenly become aware of someone walking beside them, without seeing them, a companion, a strong feeling of joy, contentment, hope for the near future. And, as the linking became stronger, those on the Earth plane, who encouraged these thoughts, developed into what you call mediums, and you have one or two of them with you today. They, over a period of time, increased their abilities. Some of them see people. Some of them hear people, people from the other side, as you call it, but they are merely souls without bodies. They are all spirits, on both sides; those with bodies and those without. That linkage, with practice and training, became more and more easy. You have seen, or you have been aware of, this linkage taking place in this group. It is all beneficial. It is good for you. It is good for anyone who is aware of the recordings of these conversations, and it is good for our group because we know that we are helping others to make progress. And that is the secret of spiritual life, to help others, without any conditions, without any demands, to help them in their advancement.

So there is the life on the other side, where I am, and at your side, where I am, where they are. We are all together, all on our own path, a path which started as a spark of light from God, and with experience and education, making progress or advancement on, and on, and on.

The sad thing is that there are so many in the dark shadows. Darkness and evil are there, but, as I have said before, you can be optimistic. You will make it. You will make the grade, to use an expression. You will get there, as I will, one day. Bless you!

P.   Antony, just before you leave us.   Over Christmas, when I was with my friends in France, I remembered your description of when the cells were conceived, and when we choose our parents, and when we visit the womb and keep on coming back.   I don't know why, but that really touched my heart.   I remembered it all over Christmas.

CHAPTER THREE

I am glad you did, because that part was, unfortunately, omitted from the recording, because of a technical fault. The operator was not fully qualified, not fully trained, and he tried to make a note of the memories, and you can hear those again. But, I remember it well.

P. It was beautiful. It came up in the conversation, not actually about that, but I did speak to a friend of mine, over the table, and he said, very sarcastically, where did you get that from? I said, I am not telling you because you would not believe it if I said.

Bring him here one night!

P. He is in France, and he is a great disbeliever. Antony, may I bless you for that, thank you.

Yes. I remember it well. The memory of those words will be locked into your computer, and will always be with you, and, on the occasions when you wish to recall it, you can ask for it to be played back to you. It was a joyful occasion. I was pleasantly surprised when you felt that you could remember that far back, and before that! Which proves the point?

P. I am getting a bit worried, because I keep on leaving things and forgetting where I put them, so you have to tick me ten out of ten for remembering that!

You can always ask one of your helpers where did you put so-and-so. They know better than you, where you left things and have forgotten them. They will tell you.

P. Yes, they have. There is one more thing that I have to ask them about. Any way, I joke with you, but I want to thank you very much.

That is a kind thought and it is good to hear it. Bless you.

C.   Do you wish to leave now?

A few minutes more?

C.   Is Arthur alright?

Yes.   He has croaked a bit.

C.   A very easy one.   I will leave the others for another week. How do you celebrate Christmas in spirit?

Simply.   We do not.   We come to the Earth plane to celebrate it with you.   We share the time with you, and, for those who have sincere beliefs, and memories, of Christ's birth, and wish to enjoy the celebrations of that day, we are with them.   There are so many, on the Earth plane, who are not celebrating Christmas, at Christmas time; they are celebrating.   But the joy of the experience of his soul, and the torment, through which he was put, are a wonderful story, memory, fact of life, which so many people belittle.   But, I would ask them, would you be nailed to a tree in order to help somebody?   Not one of them said yes. They are unkind people, and progress is made by being kind and helpful, thoughtful, sincere, with the occasional joke.   I think that I should say Farewell, and I hope to see you all next week. Bless you.

ANTONY SAYS ...
CHAPTER FOUR

My greetings to you all.   It is good to be with you again.   I see that you have questions in your minds.   Are you ready to take a step forward?

P.   Is there a law in the spirit world, or, is it up to us how many times we choose to return to the Earth plane, or, is it that we do not learn all these lessons that we need to learn, or do we come to the Earth plane until we do?

No, no, and yes.   Or something like that!

Is there a law?   We will take that one first.

For a very long period, only one visit was considered sufficient to be a testing period, for each individual, ready to prepare them for the return home, where they could continue their progress.   But, eventually, it was suggested that a second visit might be beneficial.   As you know, in this world, we do experiment, (to use the wrong word).   But you understand what we mean?   We try different systems, and we see any benefits, and the snags, in any changes of the system.   We learn from the disappointments.   That is all part of the general movement forward.   And eventually, it was found to be a good way of progress, or, a method which enabled an individual soul to maintain the momentum of progress, by having more and more periods on the Earth plane.   But, each time, each new life, in a body, it was starting with an apparent clean sheet in their memory.   Some of them continued to make the same mistakes, that they had made in previous lives in a body, without changing the system, without changing their progress, their rate of progress.   And there are other thoughts about the wisdom of multiple lives, but, each individual soul can make a recommendation for their own future by coming back again.

As you know, some of those lives were of a very short period, a few months, or a few years, and so it is understandable that not much progress was made. But now, in the last few thousand years, lives of up to one hundred years have given the opportunity of making great progress, learning from repeated mistakes in that same life, and eventually understanding why there needs to be a change in attitude, a change in direction. So, there is no law saying that you are required to have so many lives, or so many years of life, whether it is in one life, or many, on the Earth plane. It is the result of an opportunity for individual decisions to be made by a single soul: I would like to advance under those circumstances, and experience those difficulties, and adjust my attitudes, because of that experience. That is the thinking. Was there a third part to your question?

P. No, thank you, Antony. That is alright.

C. Maria is missing, tonight, and next week, because she is ill, at the moment, and so, I have a question for you. I wonder if you would like to talk to us and tell us about the aura and chakras? What is the aura made up of, for instance, what elements are used and how do they work, and why?

They are both connected. The aura, as you understand it, is an occasionally visible area, surrounding a soul in a body, or a soul, not in a body, completely surrounding it. You ask, what are the elements? The elements of an aura are not earthly elements, as you understand it. It is not of any substance of earthly matter. It is recognised in the eyes and minds of nearby spirits, whether they are in a body or not. It is a recognition of the fact that another soul is present. A soul, whose aura is being seen, is also seeing the aura of the observer. Now, the aura, not having substance, is entirely a spiritual phenomenon, it is not made of any chemicals. It is a spiritual signal for recognition, for an awareness of the soul it surrounds and contains. It is in a state of constant flux, reacting to the spiritual condition of that soul, and to the visual capabilities of the observer. It is denser nearer the soul and fading further away. It is, what you call, 'seeing someone's light'. It could be pure white. It could be a different colour, but it is more likely to be a rapidly changing multiplicity of colours, read by the observer. Another observer, nearby, might recognise different colours, simultaneously with the first observer, which indicates that the observations are in the mentality of the observers. Can you understand it up to that point?

C. I think so. You see, what comes to my mind, as you are talking, is that we should be able to read the aura. The aura is changing all the time. It is as we are. The aura changes.

I have not come to that yet. I am only describing what it is, and what it is not. It is not a chemical. It is not a physical substance. It is a sight within the mind of the observer. Two or more observers see different colours at the same time. So, it is not strictly describable. It is in a constant state of flux, moving closer and moving away from the centre of the soul it surrounds, but, being in that condition, it certainly attracts the attention of other souls. That is the first point. Each observing soul reads the pattern of colours that it observes, or believes it observes, and understands the ability to recognise that soul again, if they have met before. It is a form of recognition, but it is an indication of the condition of that soul.

P. Is it an energy, Antony? Would you call it an energy?

You would. You would call it 'an energy'. It is a constant flux.
There is, on the Earth plane, what you call, 'first impressions'. You meet a complete stranger, and a number of things can happen. You are introduced. You may, or may not, know the name of each other, but there is eye contact. You see each other; you see each other's face, features. You see the expression on their face, whether they are smiling or not. You see the refinements, or coarseness, of their features, only indicating something of their origins, but it is a form of recognition. You may feel an instant

liking, or disliking, of the other person; and that feeling can be the same for the other, it can be mutual, an instant dislike. Now, that first impression is a relic of the days when your ancestors lived much closer to nature, and they had to decide, in order to survive, whether they were going to kill and eat what they met, or whether the stranger was suitable for amalgamation into their community, a liking or a disliking. If it was a disliking, the feeling was probably mutual, and they would attack each other and the winner would feast on the flesh of the victim. That was the raw state of life, at one time.

Those sorts of feelings continue, even these days, with your so-called civilisation. You meet people, and you make a decision, or, the decision is made for you, instantly. The signals are there. Something of that is similar to seeing, or for one spirit to see, the aura of another. And, as you are spirits in a body, it can be involved in that meeting with a stranger. It is to be hoped that you do not always eat people you dislike. You laugh. You have made progress. But those were the truths. That did happen.

P. I suppose, Antony, that really we carry on with the things that we did in the 'raw state', if you know what I mean, because we do not invite people into our homes, that we don't like. So, that's like a throwback, isn't it?

It is in a trace element of the same attitudes. It is a matter of trust. If you feel an instant mistrust, of someone you meet, you do not usually warm to them, or invite them to meet your young daughter.

Now, that is a very light-hearted look at 'aura'. The technicalities of it are much further advanced than the topics that we are able to discuss, but it is involved with recognition, awareness, and it helps the observer to form an instant feeling of 'for or against'.

You asked about 'chakras', as part of the same question.

Now, if you know nothing about chakras, and you want to learn, you can read some of the many books on Eastern religions and you can be completely confused. If you know nothing about chakras, you can still make excellent progress, spiritually, without needing that awareness. But, having said that, let me give you a bit more. How many chakras would you say you have?

C. Seven.

You say seven. How would you describe one of those chakras, on your body?

C. They are like cones, that open and close. We were told, that when you do any spiritual work, they open.

I understand where you are going, now. To start with the counting; two of the chakras, the one at the top of the head, and the other at the base of the spine; they are what you could call 'vertical'. The other five chakras, on the body, are more 'horizontal', but, if you have five of these cones of yours at the front of the body, you have another five at the back of the body, in a similar position. So, do you have twelve chakras, or do you have seven? It does not matter which you say, that is the situation. You describe them as cones. They are often described as cones revolving at a very high speed, with the point of the cone at the body, and the open mouth leading away from the body. So, if you look at your chakra at your heart, there is one in the front, coming out and opening forwards, but there is a similar one on the back, in a similar position, opening out away from the back. These open chakras are a channel of communication between one spirit and another, where one of those spirits, the one with the chakras, is in an Earth body. It is really a linking between spirit away and spirit within the body, when it is open. You referred to closing the chakras, and there is a time when it is very wise to go through a procedure for closing them. Mentally, this is done starting at the top of the head and working down, closing each one, picturing it closing, picturing the revolving cone, closing and collapsing, to prevent another spirit coming in to link. But, immediately there is a link between one spirit and another one in a body, the chakras of the one in the body will open. If you have asked for protection, and gone through the procedure of closing, after a church service, or after a group meeting like this, that is wise, but, remember, a kind thought from a loved one, at a distance, can open your chakras, if a link is made, because that is the only way they can link.

So, you can have a constant state of anxiety, whether you chakras are open or closed, and that is not a good thing. It is a good thing to have this awareness of keeping protection from spirit around you, an imagined wall that is impenetrable by the dark ones, a wall built by spirit, around you, above you, and below you. But, you cannot live like that for long, because, once you send out a kind thought, a healing thought to another, you are opening your chakras! It is just one way of asking you to be aware of the risks. The constant threat from the dark forces is there, but they do not willingly come to a shining white aura, or a beautiful, multi-coloured, ever-changing aura. They do not willingly come near, unless there is an evil purpose from a much more powerful one of the dark shadows, and that is a topic on which we could spend one whole evening, talking of the horrible frighteners that are there, forever threatening!

C. and P.   I don't think so.   No, thank you, Antony.   We have enough nightmares!

But, do you understand 'striking a balance' between having protection, closing your chakras, or, having a more carefree life, just being glad of being linked with spirit, and relying on a little supervision, a little help from your often unseen helpers, who are with you constantly?

C.   The reason that I asked that was that we had been told different things, in development, in development groups, and I have learnt something tonight, the chakras open when you do prayer, anything spiritual, the chakras will open, and this is why we ask for the protection, as you pointed out, and we say the Lord's Prayer.   When I have finished the service and close, I then automatically close them to the best of my ability, and ask my spirit guides and helpers to make sure that I have closed down correctly, you understand. This is what we have been taught to do, because of the risks involved in our churches today. It is different in our home group, but not in the church. It has been instilled in us, and it is very important to do this. Tonight, you have said that, as soon as we send a kind thought, the chakras open, and, being forgetful, like I am, I often forget to close them. I have often gone through the years not doing this, not closing them at all.

I can recommend that you maintain a slightly stronger awareness of the risk, without being stressed over it, without being anxious. You are well protected. You have your own regular helpers, who are linked in their own group, with other groups, and eventually with my group. There is this awareness, and, if you are at risk, we will probably be aware of it before you. If there is an approach from evil ones, with intent to harm you and or your family, we are almost certain to be aware before you, and protection will be there. There have been occasions, as you know, where there has been a movement to try to stop you doing your good work, in and out of churches. We have been fully aware, and, usually, we move at sufficient speed to prevent your becoming aware. Occasionally, that has not happened and you have noticed interference, but do not worry.

You mentioned the Lord's Prayer. That is one of the most beautiful, well-constructed prayers to the Creator, that has ever been said, ever been given to you, and it puzzles me, really puzzles me, why there are so many, in this movement of awareness of spiritual life, who do not like to use the Lord's Prayer. They are harming themselves, by depriving themselves of the protection, 'Deliver us from evil'. That is a very clear-cut request for protection, which is always granted, always reinforced, because it may be in existence, anyway. But, that is freedom of choice. There are those who will not accept, either Jesus or his prayer. That is their choice. And, one day, they may well have the opportunity to explain it to him, why they rejected him. That is freedom of choice. You have made the choice of wanting to use that prayer, and that is good. You will not have to explain your dislike for it, but others will.

C. We have visited many churches, of late, that do not take Jesus Christ as the son of God. They will not allow the Lord's Prayer to be spoken.

Yes. I am aware.

C. Sometimes, I have said it on my own, because nobody else wanted to say it; they don't think it is necessary after the opening prayer. I have said, it is a form of protection for us and, if you don't mind, I am going to say it on my own. So, here again, it is a man-made decision, and this is why the spiritualist movement is weak, because it is split. We prefer to go into the Christian churches, more so than the others who have a different way of viewing spirit. As they say, Jesus Christ was one of the greatest mediums and healers of all time, but there were also others, Mohamed, Buddha, and so forth. It is a different attitude, shall we say. Not all churches are like this, but there are a few that are very rigid, so we choose really not to serve them because we are not happy. I am not happy doing it because I'm not relaxed, because I'm afraid of standing without the protection, which I ask for, constantly.

You are not without that protection. You have only to think, 'Deliver us from evil', and that is a request for protection. That message is received and acted upon. You have mentioned some of these churches and their rules. There are some, that you have visited, where they have been told not to say the Lord's Prayer, and then they say, we will sing it, instead! That shows that there are members of that church who are not accepting the questionable dogma being sent to them. And, that is a healthy sign. It is a good sign.

CHAPTER FOUR

In all those churches, that you visit, there are many, in both the two groupings you mentioned, where darkness visits, where members of the congregation, and/or members of the committees running those churches, organising those services, bring 'passengers of darkness' with them. You must have felt it?

C.   Oh, yes. I have been very aware of that.

All the more reason to ask for protection that can help prevent those dark entities from affecting the service, or affecting those in the congregation. It is sad, it is bad, that it happens, but, you can take the light into those churches and drive the darkness out, even if it is only for that one service. Let them feel the upliftment, and the joy of linking with spirit in the best possible way. You do it. Many do it. The difficulty is where those in authority become 'carriers'. Is it not a good thing, to link with them, and wish them well, send them healing, surround them with a white light, and help to drive that bad spirit away? Is that not a good way of dealing with the problem?

C.   I think so, yes. I think that is the only way.

It is. I understand that those who are affected by the darkness carry it with them, but they need all the love and help that can be sent to them, even if they react in an unpleasant way and can be unkind in return. That is their problem, not yours. If you can help them to be rid of that passenger, that is another step forward. That is advancement for you, and for them.
Have you any more questions?

C.   Actually, you have answered the other question that I had, because it was 'How do we recognise another spirit?' That led on to that.

I must have been reading your mind!

C.   Oh, yes.   I see.

If I took my transition, tonight, and I am sure that you would not want me to, but, you would not want to be meeting up with me yet, I am sure.   If I took my transition tonight, and entered the spirit world, it might help Phyllis as well as myself, how would I recognise one of my family?   We talked about the aura and the colours, but how would they recognise me and how would I recognise them and the friends that I have met in the past?

Let me say that you are not going to take your transition tonight. We are not ready for you.   You were talking about taking your transition and meeting me.   I meet you every week.   I meet you every day. I see you. I recognise you. You recognise me, either with a picture in your mind, or a thought in your mind, or just a name in your mind.   You have seen your parents, your brother; you have seen other loved ones who have taken their transition already.   You have recognised them in your dreams, have you not?   That is how you will recognise your loved ones when you go to spirit, when you return to the world of spirit and our peculiar timing system.   You will know them instantly; they will know you.   You will see them in your mind.   You will take your third eye with you.   You will leave the other two behind, because they are closed.   There is joy in the instant recognition. They will know that you are coming.   They will be waiting to guide you, when you go through that tunnel, that you talk and think about, the tunnel, that you can get through and then come back again.   Most people, taking their transition, go through and emerge into the sunshine and the beautiful countryside awaiting them.

P.   I am glad that you mentioned about the tunnel, Antony.   It always put a little bit of fear into me, I don't know why, but it does, and I'm pleased.

You call it a tunnel.   It is not a tunnel.

CHAPTER FOUR

P.   Oh, I'm pleased, bless you, thank you.

It is the point of changing from the darkness of this world into the glories, and beauties, and peace, and opportunities for advancement in the spirit world.   It appears to be like a tunnel. Those who have had serious operations, and have had their heart stopped beating, have had a dream of going through a tunnel. They see the light ahead of them.   Some of them put their head out into the sunshine, and they are tugged backwards, because their cord has not been broken.   They are still 'of the world'. The physical link is still there with the body, and they are tugged back.   They, in their little computers, have recognised that they have come out of the tunnel into sunshine, only to be drawn back again.   They are disappointed.

P.   I have heard that.

It is very disappointing, once you have seen it.   You can only make progress, after that.   You will enjoy it, shaking off the tired old bodies, all the pains, difficulties, you know it, you've seen some of them.   You may not have any more pain, but, the memories of it will be there and you will be glad to be relieved. With the joy of seeing those loved ones, there is no question of 'how will I recognise them'; you won't be able to help yourself. It is a little over-whelming.   And that is just before you face your own computer records!   There's the shock!   But, it is all part of progress.   It is good.

C.   Does that apply to our lovely animals, our pets, when they take their transition?

Yes.   They do move on different levels.   They have limitations of mental capacity, which you are aware of, on the Earth plane, and you are still aware of it at the other side, at our side.   But, you have the control.   If you wish them to be with you, they are there.   If you wish to comfort or stroke them, they are there.

You might not feel the texture, physically, because you do not have hands, but the comfort and reassurance, and the look in their eyes, as they recognise you, is delightful.

P. I shall meet my little budgie again.

C. The etheric body...

That is a contradiction of terms.   A body means something physical. Etheric means something ethereal.   So, a spirit body is an imaginary body in the mind and the eye of the beholder. That body can be what the spirit wishes. Most people, following a life in a body on Earth, if they live the fullness of time, do not wish to retain the tired old body; they like to appear youthful, full of life, which they are; but, they are not youthful. They may be thousands of years old, or more, but it is the impression they give of being a young, vital, spirit, that is recognisable by those loved ones who shared some of their time on Earth.   They may look young, very attractive, for the best possible reasons.

C. I think I may go back to my Egyptian time.

You were a very smart looking girl, then, and you used it.   You used your appearance, then, to attract attention and demand obedience.

C. Yes. I know I was not very good then.

All part of the learning curve, or curves!

Laughter, pause...

C. Are you still with us?

A. He is still here. Why was I jerked back?

CHAPTER FOUR

Yes. The link is still here.

C. Do you wish to continue, Antony?

If you have further questions.

C. Was there a break there?

Yes.

C. Just one point about healing, spiritual healing.
Sometimes, it seems as if the healing is not working, or there is not any relief. Is this because the person, who is going through the illness, needs to experience that illness to gain spiritual growth and understanding, or is it because the link was not made properly with the guides?

It could be either of those two or other points. You are getting good at asking questions and then giving me the answers; and you are quite right. It is possible, that the soul concerned is required to go through that physical experience, because they have chosen to do so, to learn from it. There might be some slight adjustment, or alteration in their attitudes, required before they can make further progress, that can only be introduced into their state of awareness by going through that physical experience, which can be painful, which is testing, but is beneficial. So, that is a possibility. It is also possible that the wrong link, or an incomplete link, is made by the healer, when asking for relief, from that pain, for that patient. That is always possible.

But, you can always, as a healer, do what Arthur has done, and ask to be shown the cause of that problem. And then, you may be shown it, or you may not be shown it, depending on the correctness of that system. You know, from his experience, that spirit can actually indicate another cause, or the main cause of that condition in that patient. Spirit can give to the healer an awareness of the problem, what is wrong. It is sometimes shown as a dark mark, a dark arrowhead, for want of a better description, for pain, or even for a growth, which is creating a problem. That knowledge is there for the healer and not for the patient. The healer should not tell the patient what they have seen. It is educational, and it is helpful to the healer to have some idea of the problem. It might appear in a different area from where the patient feels the pain. That can happen. It can be muscular pain. It can be in the nervous system only. It can be caused by problems in the alimentary tract, in the bowel, the lack of strength in the automatic muscles of the bowel system, a lack of strength caused by poor diet, which can create pockets, as you are aware, that have been dealt with, pockets which can fill and be packed with material; material, which should be passed down the bowel, is held back in a pocket to create pain. These sorts of things can be shown to the healer to help him or her to urge spirit to manipulate and empty those pockets, if that is the main cause, and so on.

C. Yes. That has been done through psychic surgery.

Yes. That is psychic surgery, without a knife.

C. And nothing shows on an x-ray, then, does it?

No.

C. It is a wonderful thing.

That can be shown to the healer, as you know. The healer can make further progress helping that patient, because he or she has that knowledge.

C. Yes. Right. I think we have covered quite a lot tonight, Antony.

P. Bless you, Antony

CHAPTER FOUR

I will look forward to seeing you between now and next week; and especially next week.

C. I hope so. We do thank you for coming, and using Arthur. I think Arthur is a bit under the weather, and I am sure you are aware of that?

I will see you next week.   Ask for protection.

ANTONY SAYS ...
CHAPTER FIVE

My greetings to you.   It is good to be with you again.   It is hoped that the two absentees will soon be able to rejoin you.

C. We hope so.   We thought we would continue just the same, Antony, because, whatever we ask will be recorded, and we can play it back to them when they return.   Do you still want me to ask questions?

Yes, continue by all means, and if these recordings are clear, they can be heard by, or read to, many others in the future.

C. Right, what are the different stages of advancement from the level that you are on at the moment and from the level that we are on, and how are these stages monitored?

You have been having some deep thoughts and you deserve an answer to these questions.
    What are the stages and how are they monitored?

C.   Yes.   At our level and at your level.

You wish to start at your level?

C.   Yes

What I am going to say will apply to progress from any one level to the next one, so from your level to the next one, we can look at that. You, throughout your life on the Earth, on this occasion, have been aware of certain basic tendencies that are with you, part of you, and that affect your attitude to all others with whom you come in contact.   They are the basic facts of your life; for example, you believe in self protection in order for your life to continue without too much damage to yourself. Your instincts enable you to react instantly, when you are threatened physically. This applies to the majority of those at your level. Without it, you would not have a long life, and it is possible that your life would be shortened in the early stages. Do you understand that so far?

C. Yes.

That is one instinct that is built into you. At much higher levels than yours, that instinct has been, firstly, controlled, secondly suppressed, and thirdly, eliminated. This is not particularly at the next level to you, but soon after your level. There are some at your level who are suppressing the instinct. That is accepting the condition of the termination of your life, in the knowledge that others wish you harm and that you do not wish them harm for having those thoughts. That is a big step to take. And there are many other steps forward similar to that where the reaction, the automatic reaction, is there within you, and which you apply at any similar situation where your well-being is threatened, and it is natural to look after your property, your family, to defend yourself, your friends, your neighbours. It is part of a state defensive system for young people to willingly join the armed forces of their own nation, in order to accept orders from their superior officers to do whatever is required by the orders of those officers, to defend their country, even if it means invading another country and attacking the occupants. That tendency is given names like "patriotism", and enthusiasm from governing bodies encourages young people to react to that patriotic tendency to go out and do harm to others, under their instruction. So, another step forward could be looked upon as the weakening of the patriotic resolve, which is probably as tidy a way of saying it as possible. You understand that second point?

C. Yes. Is it just the defence of oneself, because there are many points that I would like to bring up now that you have explained. There must be more things that you have to go through or endure, before you can move up a stage, than that one thing?

That is why, in the phraseology being used, I do not like the word "levels". The understanding and recognition of progress in spiritual advancement, which is what we are talking about, is in a constant state of flux, moving forward. Some people make no progress for a time and appear to go backwards, but they do, in fact, make no progress. We are looking at positive progress as a way of measurement, or understanding, of the development. So, where a person decides to harm, kill, destroy, damage, (or whatever word you wish), another soul, thinking that they are defending themselves, they are not moving forward with that action, because damage to the surroundings of another soul, hurting them, killing them, deliberately creating problems for them, in order to have that feeling of greater security, and personal satisfaction at having had, what might be called, revenge for some other damage in the other direction, that can be harmful. That is on the record for both the souls concerned, and it delays their progress, but it is much easier to talk about progress of one pace from where you are, that you have achieved up to now, than to talk about moving seven stages higher, or five stages higher, or whatever the number of stages involved. It is far too complicated to try to put fifty million years experience into one hour. It cannot be done. We do not try to do it, and that is why we cannot give you the complete answer in a book or in a library of books. We can only show you the direction to go, and help you with your philosophies, your thinking, of improving your desire to progress. That is a stage. There are many souls who enjoy being on the sort of advancement or stage that you are. They enjoy the comforts of a family life, the friendships, the messages, the chatter. It can be quite a comfortable way of living, but it does not last for ever. As time passes, the body becomes more weary, and there is a period when it is necessary to return home and you take your transition. Now, if that transition is taken by physical violence from an outsider, from another, probably affected by an evil influence, robbing and murder, that sort of violence gives a great temptation to resist, and you have that right, that ability to protect yourself, given to you by your government. It is a natural instinct in many people and it is not easy to remove that instinct and accept damage from another, which could terminate the life and give reason for your return home.

It is not easy, but, somewhere between the stage at which you are now, and the higher, future, levels, you will need to weaken that determination to survive at all costs. It will happen, but not in this life. It may not be in the next, or however many lives are ahead of you, until you reach a point where you have advanced so far that there is no real benefit in coming back to experience another life on this, or any other, planet. It is a long, long way ahead, but there is time for it. Eternity gives you time for it. In our group, we have all been through the lower levels and worked our way up. We know that we went through experiences of hate and lust and killing, and we have made progress from that stage, step by step. It is a very long process, nothing to worry about. You are showing a very strong resolve to make progress, by asking these questions, by continuing with this dialogue that we are having through the voice and vocabulary of Arthur. You are showing a very strong determination to advance, and you are to be congratulated. But, do not feel despondent when you know that you may have, or you may feel, the need to have thoughts of reacting to the aggressive advance from another, or to look for, and promise yourself, revenge for damage done to you, through no fault of your own. These are all indications of stages of advancement, and you will move on. Does that help you?

C. Yes. Actually, this question, as you might know, came from Arthur!

No! And you tell me now?

C. Yes, and he asked me to ask because it is something he wanted to know, and when we play it back, he will hear it and ...

He may have other questions?

C. Yes.

Which he can ask another day?

C. Yes. When you were talking, you said that you had been through all these stages, and been tested all the way along. At one stage of my life, if someone hurt me or my family, I immediately wanted revenge. I have now, I feel, moved on from that. If someone hurts me now, and I know that I have people around me, who smile at me to my face, and would wish me harm behind my back, but, I am beginning to learn that I can, in a sense, forgive, because of their own ignorance and failing. At one time I could not, but now, when I am deeply hurt by somebody, and they say that they are friends with me, and they are a sincere friend, and I find that they are not actually at all times sincere, I find that I can overlook it. Sometimes I fail, and I have to say my piece; another time I can forgive and let it go, especially within my own family, I can. If they say, forgive me, I can forgive.

You are to be congratulated. You had learned some things long before I came in contact with you here and you have made progress. You are aware, or you were aware, of the need for forgiveness. You gave it a great deal of thought. You worked on that process. You developed yourself to the point where you gave forgiveness. And one way in which you can help yourself to forgive is to remember that, when you have an awareness of unkind thoughts from your so-called friends, where in the past you would have hit back at them, given them what Arthur would have called a tongue-lashing, now, you think 'oh, poor dear, they are in a bad way, they are physically or mentally in a bad way and need help', and you send them a kind thought. That takes away all that desire for revenge, and that is true progress. That makes it so much easier to take that big step, and it is a very big step to take, moving away from having thoughts of revenge, to having thoughts of healing. The change was in you. They are the ones with the problem. Their problem is now even bigger.

CHAPTER FIVE

We did not mention, or I did not give you any response to your enquiry, about monitoring progress. I have given it to you before in talks about that little, (and very big), computer, within yourself, which logs or records every thought, every word you say, every word you read, every picture you see every experience, especially those where you are making progress, and that is logged within you and, on your return home, when you review your experiences of your Earth-life, it is noted that you have a 'flower in your garden', to use one of your expressions, for each of those deeds. It is noted that those flowers, as you always say, are beautiful and they last forever. So there, you have it. You are aware of your improving, increasing awareness of methods of making progress. You are very much aware.

C. I do try because I ...

And you succeed.

C. Not always. Now and again, I am afraid I slip back ...

But the recognition that you slip back is progress. When you had thoughts of revenge, as a young person, you had no regrets. You let your expressions flow, so that they were heard, but now, if you do express yourself in an unkindly way, you hear it and you are aware of it and you criticise yourself for it. That is progress. The growing awareness of, what you might call slight misdemeanours and wrong-thinking, negative thinking, is progress. So, you are already moving forward, tonight, when you realise that you have that awareness of your own progress!

C. I have learned that I upset myself too much, because I know I have not had a kind thought for somebody or, perhaps, I have not done all I could have done for them, and they have criticised me when I have tried to do my best, and I have ended up in tears because it hurts me so much. When I was younger, and did not know all these things, it did not hurt me. But now I am older,

61

and have experienced more in this life, and it has been a difficult life, parts of it, especially with the sickness with the children and my parents, myself, and everybody else, I have changed. I am getting on a more even keel, shall we say, to what I was. I am calmer, but I do get very upset. I think that is because, doing the spiritual work I am getting more sensitive.

Yes. That is always possible. As you are changing, as your awareness improves, and your progress is maintained, each day you can be a little bit further forward than the previous day, but it does bring, with the increasing awareness of your progress, an increasing awareness of negativity, and that can be weakening. That can affect your emotions. And then you feel, I want to be strong and tough again, I do not want to feel like this.

It is not right that you should feel like that. So, it is a case of, first of all getting the protection again, always keep asking for protection, then sending out those healing thoughts of white light to the one causing the stress, and asking spirit for help to survive any attack on your emotions, because these attacks do come, they are part of the natural reaction for revenge, from those who have the unpleasant thoughts. They send negative thoughts to you, and, if you can build a barrier with your protection of yourself, the spiritual protection, the help from all your helpers, from your family, who are with you at difficult times, all those around you, and you feel the strength of them around you, then you will not go down. This is where fighting comes in. You can fight against these spiritual attacks, and that is where you can continue to fight.

In my group, we are fighters. We are fighters against evil. Instead of fighting against others who do not agree with us, we fight against evil in whatever form we find it. And that is good! So, that is positive. So, you can be a fighter and be positive and make progress.

C. Another question that might interest our two friends, when they come back, is about reincarnation. I think that we touched

CHAPTER FIVE

on this in the beginning, before they joined us, but it might be of interest to them, if you wouldn't mind going through it again. When we reincarnate, do we reincarnate into the same family, the same family group. Very often we have been told, Oh yes, you could have been my brother, or, Yes, I was probably your daughter, you know, when we meet up again in the family group; or do we reincarnate into an entirely new family group?

The answer is, Yes, to all of them. With the many incarnations that you have had, and you have had many, you try them all. The family group, as you call it; there is a physical family group on the Earth plane for one life, but then you may meet up with some of those spirits in another life. It is easy to feel recognition. When you are contemplating another life on the planet, you have plenty of time to look around, plenty of time to listen to advice from more experienced souls from higher levels, if you want that word, more experienced souls, more advanced souls, to suggest that you look here, look there, and you ask yourself, what are you looking for, anyway? Are you looking for a new experience, of some sort or other? You can ask them, what will help me to advance? You can ask spirit at any time, what will help me to advance? You will get some sort of help, some answer. Here you are getting a lot of words, from the experience of a lot of souls, in a lot of different groups. They are all linked, as you know, and the groups that you joined for advancement, when you were at this side of 'the divide', as you call it, have all linked with other groups above them, that are more experienced, more advanced, than they are. Your own guides and helpers who are with you, and there is always someone with you, they have all had experiences, and they can give you an instant answer, if you open your mind for it. So, there is no need to have anxieties about family groups. It is all experience. You may go into a group, where your brothers, sisters, are good friends to you, or where they are not good friends to you. You will learn from both types of family. You might go where the earthly parents are happy together, or miserable together, and you will learn

63

from both types of parenting. There is an unlimited amount that you can learn, but the basic facts, which you have asked for before, are the laws of the godhead and the need to want to help others. If you remember those facts, when you have a disappointing friendship, smother them with light. Wish them well. Feel sorrow for them, in their bad choice of words, their bad decisions to hurt you or hurt others. Bless them. Make it difficult for them to be unpleasant. You can do it from a distance. They do not need to see you. They have no need to know what you are saying, doing, or sending out for them. They will feel the effect of it and they will wonder what is happening to them. It will make them think, and then, like you, they may say, I have been on the wrong path, or I have done this incorrectly, or, I would like to help others. Does that help you?

C. Yes. Thank you. I have another question here for you. Why are bodily illnesses related to colours in healing? Is this to do with the aura? Or, when we did colour healing, we were shown the different colours to pass through the body, and we wonder whether certain colours are related to the body?

The illnesses do not create the colour. The healer creates the colours to help the illness, or the negativity. Illness does not dictate at all. Illness is a negative, physical condition, which can be helped medically, spiritually; it can be helped, but the help is positive thought sent from spirit. It may be a spirit, within an earthly body, who has been trained to heal, and can do it, and bring help and benefit to the patient. But the illness of that patient, the problems, the physical, chemical and mental problems, within that patient, do not dictate how they can be healed, they are not looking for healing, they are not having thoughts. It is a condition which can get better or get worse, and can create other side effects. It can create a terminal condition. Many people die, return home. They take their transition because the negativity of the illness becomes so serious that it affects the organs, which fail to function properly. But those conditions do not dictate

CHAPTER FIVE

anything about colour. They react to spiritual colour sent to them from a healer, whether the healer is in a body or not. Now, there is a choice of colours for healing, and, here again, we do experiment from this side, many experiments have been carried out in colour healing, and you were trained to mentally pass healing colours through the body of a patient who needs healing. The patient lying down, the hands on the head, the hands of other helpers, supporters, at the feet or around the side, or on the site of the damage, those healing colours, reinforced by the healing thoughts of the supplementary healers, those at the side and at the feet, create a tremendous, powerful flow of healing colour, of the chosen colour, through the body, for a short period. There is a tremendous surge of well-being throughout the patient. I can feel it now. It is there in this body. It is good. Little points of damage are helped, and the colours that are passed through, you were trained in a sequence, which is a good thing, which builds up a routine in your mind, which you never forget. And in that healing sanctuary, where it is regularly practised, great benefit is received, sometimes received by those who are about to take their transition. Maybe, they were due to take it anyway, but they feel so much more relaxed. They feel the benefits of that healing. It is very well worthwhile. Those who have had it, and then gone to spirit, because their time was up, have looked back on that period, before their transition, with appreciation to those who gave it, and they have helped to strengthen their resolve to continue sending out healing thoughts. The colours are dictated by the healer, not by the patient. Colours vary; with different healers sending out what they think is the same colour, creating variations. But, there is no harm in that. All the different variations of the colour are beneficial, in some way or other. So, where you have three or four healers around one patient, sending out what they think is the same colour, it can greatly strengthen the effect of the healing received from the passage of that colour or the varying shades of that colour. There is no signal from a disease demanding a colour.

C. No. I understand that. Perhaps, I put that wrongly to you. I understand about the colour healing and how it works. How about when we just lay on the hands, and when the energy that we feel coming through our hands to the patient, that is not colour, is it? That is an energy, isn't it?

Not always. Sometimes a colour is sent, but there may not be an awareness of the colour by the healer, whose hands are on the patient. The spiritual healers, working through that healer, know if they are sending a colour. They know if a colour is beneficial.

The strongest colour of all is, as you know, a near-white, but that contains all colours. White is a blending of all colours of the spectrum. You see it in your rainbow. That is white light, broken into different colours. Put all those colours together again and you have white light. So, if you are sending a white light signal through a patient, they can pick whatever colour helps most. Or, it can be picked for them.

C. As you say, we are only a channel of healing energy. As far as we are concerned it is important only that we are able to help somebody.

That's right. You are making progress! You know these things!

C. One more thing. Transfiguration. I once saw this in church, where they did the mouldings on the medium's face, and you can recognise a loved one from spirit. I found this to be quite unusual, very interesting to watch. What are these mouldings? How do they build on to a face? We were told to keep talking, because the voices kept the mouldings going. If we didn't speak they seemed to fade very quickly.

Yes. This was another example of spiritual experiments. Over the centuries, spirits, particularly those who had returned home after a period on Earth, had felt a very strong urge to link with the spirits of their loved ones who remained on Earth, in a body. There was a very strong feeling and desire to let their loved ones know that they are very much alive, feeling so much better, in a happy place, feeling well, after having shaken off the earth body. This desire to renew the contact with the loved ones on the Earth plane became so strong that the more experienced spirits, or groups of spirits, agreed that we should try to link, so that communication could be regained. And now, you look back and you see what happened. There are stories of the 'knockings' in a house, tapping, or a sequence of taps, repeated spiritually, to prove that there was an intelligence aware of the sound. And this was wonderful.

But, when you compare it with what is happening tonight, here, now, it was very disappointing. Here and now, you are hearing my thoughts, instantly, translated from my mind, in my language, into the brain and vocabulary of one sitting with you. There may be times when you think that I pause for thought, or pause for breath, and there is only the slightest delay in the transfer of my thoughts through all that rigmarole, into your ears, where you hear it and understand it in your brain. Isn't that an improvement on the early stages of communication? You are aware from your own abilities as a clairvoyant, as a medium, as you say, as a channel, of receiving thoughts, pictures, words, sounds, possibly smells, but certainly sounds, from detached spirits who wish to communicate with someone who is in the room with you in your group, your church, or a community centre or village hall. You know the difficulties of linking, but you achieve it, you do it regularly, you do it instantly, to varying degrees of success, depending on the amount of power given to you at that time. The building up of the face of a loved one, on the features of another person in the room, so that the features can be recognised as the features of the grandmother, the mother, the wife, loved one, father, husband, brother, sister, who has apparently 'died', to see their features in the room, can be a wonderful experience. It can convince the observer that their loved one is still alive and is there with them now.   But, they are not there in 'body'.   They appear to be there in body, in the features.   Is that what you call 'transfiguration'?

C.   Yes.

It was one of many methods, many experiments to help the spirit world link with Earth planet, and with the spiritual souls who are in earth bodies, and who yearn for news of their lost loved ones.   It was not easily done.   It was very complicated, I think the word was 'convoluted', or a word like that, it was certainly a complicated method of convincing one observer that a loved one was in the room with him or her.   You do not hear much of it these days.   Occasionally, people experiment, trying to recreate those conditions.   They sometimes experiment, on the Earth plane, trying to recreate the conditions of messages coming by tapping and knocking.   But, is it not much easier to visit a clairvoyant, or to join a group with the ability and the experience of linking directly with spirit in this way?   Can you answer that?

C.   Yes, I can, because I have come up against it many, many times.   People fear communication.   They want it.   They want proof, but they fear it, and it puts barriers up.   It is very difficult for a medium to break those barriers down.   I think that there is more awareness now on the Earth plane.   I think the younger element are more open minded to things, but there is still that resistance to give of themselves, to give the power to help their loved ones come through.   You ask for it.   You ask for their love and their understanding, and they just look at you.   You ask for it again and they say Yes, and yet there isn't any power, and there isn't a lot of love, and yet they expect you to give them their parents' names or their husband's names, where they lived, how old they were when they died, and all sorts of things like that.   Until you are half way through the meeting, and people begin to relax, and we have a bit of laughter, then, we begin to get the evidence that we are happy with.

CHAPTER FIVE

But that shows the benefit of your experience, as a medium, of building up that rapport with those people, some of whom may well be youngsters, young people, wondering where they can go to pass an hour, where they can go for a laugh, wondering if it will be an experience that they might enjoy, or they might not enjoy, and having very little experience, very little progress on their own path. They may be very early souls, so, the best way to help them is to wish them well, as you do. Enjoy a laugh with them, and encourage them to have a laugh with you, as you do. That is your experience, and you succeed. They can be testing times, especially if you are tired, but, you will win through. You will, if you get only one completely satisfying sentence to one person in that room, you will have performed an excellent service for spirit. So, do not criticise yourself. If there is a weakness, it is in the resolve of those coming and sitting in the room with you. They, at least, are willing to open their minds and their ears to hear what is to be heard, and you gave them plenty to hear.

It was a success. There was more than one person very pleased to have been there, because of the way you were able to link with one of their loved ones. So have no regrets. The problems, the faults, are with the others, not with you. You must build on your great strength, your abilities. You should have no anxieties about whether the meeting has been a success or not. Have we any more?

C. No, I think that is quite enough for tonight. We have covered a lot of subjects.

Then I wish your two friends well, and hope that they will be here for me to welcome them next week.

C. I hope so. I will be running out of questions.

I doubt it. I can find you some questions. I can start questioning you and them. I can give them an examination. I can ask them if they have been doing their homework, whilst away from school.

C.   I do thank you, once again, and all your helpers, who are with you.   We try to do our best, and hope that we are going forward, as you say, and trying to be positive.

You are already learning.   You know that I am not just one spirit. You are linking, not with just one group of spirits, but with all the linked groups, who are all making progress, of which you are part.   Bless you!

ANTONY SAYS ...
CHAPTER SIX

It is becoming quite like old times. Welcome to the returning two ladies. You have not missed anything that you cannot hear, or read, in the future, so you will be kept up to date. It is hoped that you will ask questions, and I ask Carole to open with the first one.

C. Good evening, Antony. How can you experience pain and suffering, in spirit, without reincarnating on the Earth plane?

Quite easily. Those of us in spirit, in our linked groups, as you know, are aware of the pain and suffering inflicted on those souls on the Earth plane. We can experience that, by sharing time with them, by sharing the body space with them, and you can understand that. But, those in the spirit world, who are also receiving pain and suffering, are in a slightly different situation. The pain is an awareness of negative conditions, in the spirit world. The feeling of pain is a memory from an Earth life. The awareness is in the present tense with those who suffer. The pain, or the feelings of pain, the suffering, is felt by those to whom unkind thoughts are sent. There is a saying, on the Earth, do not speak ill of the dead, and that is worth a little thought. That expression originated from one with an awareness that the dead cannot answer back. They are dead, gone, they do not exist; which, you know, is quite incorrect, but, the thought was there. It was an honest thought that, if the dead cannot answer criticisms, negative thoughts, from those remaining on the Earth plane, it is unfair to send those unkind thoughts after them. But, that is all on the side. Those spirits, those free spirits, who feel pain and suffering, can start that feeling on their return home, when their little computer memory is poured out before them, when they realise the hurt they have created during their Earth life. The physical pain, the destruction, the unkindness, that they have sent out, given out, to others, because they wished to assert their own will, creates so much pain, resentment, creates the desire for revenge, which we have talked about, which, in sequence, increases the unpleasantness and the pain. The souls who have been hurt, or damaged, with such resentful actions, add to the confusion, feel again the suffering, as they see the picture of it from their own log of memories. So that can be the start of receiving or feeling pain or suffering. As others, who have been involved with those souls during a lifetime, return home, they, again, will revive those feelings, creating more pain, more suffering, which is felt spiritually. It is felt, not just in the memories of the souls concerned, but also with the souls who are linked with them, in either a loose group, or a tight group of souls, which we have discussed before. The tendency is for souls to group together, to work together, and to make progress together. Those groups, in the natural order of things, linked with other groups on the same or similar stages of advancement, or levels, are also linked with groups of higher stages, more advanced levels. All those linked groups, if you can picture them, spread throughout the universe, as all linked into the formation of spirit, and what you call spirit. They are all aware of that pain and suffering. They feel it. They send out healing thoughts to the root of the cause. They work upon it. That is the nature of things. So, although we do not have muscular pain, nervous pain, the physical pain, that you imagine whilst in a body, where you can feel it, there is still an awareness of pain and suffering through the thinking processes and the linkages between spirits and groups of spirits. As you might imagine, God is fully aware of it. Does that answer your question?

C. Yes, thank you. Would you like another question, now, from Maria?

Yes, please.

M. My question is about the embodiment of a divine soul. Can you tell us something about that?

CHAPTER SIX

'The embodiment of the divine soul'?

M.   Yes.   Souls, because there is more than one.

Let me give you some definitions. Your soul, my soul, every soul, whether in a body or not, is a divine spark from the Creator, God given. You cannot destroy it; no one can destroy it. That spark is given the eternal right to make decisions on its own activities, so, by definition, all souls are divine. Now, the embodiment of a soul is, to me, a description of that divine spark making its home in a human embryo, and becoming a person on this planet. So what is your question?

M.   What can you tell me about those holy men, in different parts of the world, Germany, and India, for example, where they live in an ashram, teaching and healing those who visit.   They are described as 'divine souls'.   In what way are they different from other people?   I'm sorry that I cannot remember their names.

Let me start to answer you.

You are aware that my thoughts are in a totally different language from yours. You are hearing my thoughts in the voice and vocabulary of one of your group, who has practised this form of communication, with a good degree of success, but with certain limitations. I have a thought, in my own language, you hear it in English, you reply in English, and that is brought back to me with a link, through the vocabulary, the memory, the brain, of Arthur, which is then translated into my language, and I understand you; all this instantly! That is the communication link operating now. So, unless the question you ask is in the vocabulary and memory of Arthur, it will be lost. I will not receive it, and I am not receiving it. He is aware and, through that, I am aware that, in the sub-continent of India, which is now three nations rather than one, there have been many wise men, and women, who have meditated and linked with spirit, and communicated with spirit, and helped to form groups amongst those souls in bodies living there, or travelling there. Not far from the place you were talking of, there was a different linkage, located between India and China, but it took place in the monasteries in the Tibetan mountains. There, again, you had wise men, spiritually linked, who became aware of possibilities of communication, such as you are having now. People from other countries went to India, they went to Tibet; they went to meet these gurus, to spend time with them, and to try to acquire the peace of mind that they appeared to have. And, to some degree, they succeeded; but many failed. The knowledge of their existence was recorded, was spread by word of mouth, and those individual souls, who linked directly with spirit, were able to pass on the knowledge, gained from that communication, to others, on the Earth plane, who felt that they were in the presence of servants of God, which, you could say, was true, and is true now. For the individual names about which you are asking, you need to link with, or read about, those who have studied the particular town or place, or person, whose names you have mentioned. I cannot give you any more answer because of the limitations. Do you understand?

M. Through the link, and through the meditation, they have become God-like and be able to X-ray, that's love and knowledge and understanding of each of their followers and others. Is that so?

That is so, not only in the parts that you mention but in many other parts of the world. You mention X-rays. There are healers, in this area, who are shown what is inside a body. They do not use X-rays but they have the benefit of seeing, through their third eye, the source of a problem, a medical problem, in a patient. When I tell you that all roads lead to heaven, you can imagine how many thousands, or hundreds of thousands, or millions of paths there are; all different, all going in the right direction.

CHAPTER SIX

M. Is it possible for me, or any of us, to become anywhere like those people I have mentioned? Could we achieve it, or could I achieve it? Or is it not meant for us, this time around?

You have asked me four or five questions. Could you achieve it? I would say that your aim is to achieve it. It is the aim of all of us involved in spirit, all linked, and we each have that awareness of each other's thoughts, wishes; we all have that desire to make progress to the point of perfection. The type of soul, that you have mentioned, the type that you have on your mind, with or without names, are all aiming at perfection. If you study them, it may help you, but the surest way of achieving perfection is to make progress over the period of time necessary, to the point where you will pass the stage of advancement of my group, and of others, who are more advanced, to that point of perfection.

That is the ultimate bliss, the joy of following the guide lines up to that great white light of spirit, which is ahead of us all, which is the bliss of perfection, the reunification with your Creator. And that is the end of eternity!

We are all aiming for that. We are all striving. And the purpose of this communication, with you and your friends, is to help you look in the right direction, move in the right direction, and keep moving.

So, in answer to your question, yes; you, and they, and all the souls in existence, have the opportunity to reach perfection. As you know, many do not follow that opportunity, all the time. Does that help you?

M. Yes.

C. Would you like another question now, Antony?

Yes, please.

P. Good evening, Antony. On reading the book, that Arthur wrote, I would like to ask a question, because, when I read that the people, who have to be the observers for, maybe, a hundred years, or a thousand years, are all referred to as a male. It is a puzzle to me. Please could you explain why no female is in the group? I mean this sincerely.

Yes. I can. To start with, you have given me a male name, Antony. You hear a male voice, Arthur's voice.

P. Yes. That I understand.

Even I refer to Antony as he.

P. Yes, that's quite true.

In your language, you refer to 'he' for men, and 'she' for a female.
  Well, I am neither.

P. I began to wonder when I was reading the book, but I thought, well, I haven't got any answers, any questions for you, but I thought, if he can stand it, I will ask this one.

Let me go on. From somewhere between the stages, where you and your group are, and the stages where I am, with my group, there comes a time when it is of no further benefit to return to the planet for another life. And it is only on the planet that sex has a purpose. When you were reading the book, you will recall it has a strong purpose on the planet. In the early stages, it was vital that replacements for the casualties could be created, and developed, to the point of having the strength to continue the fight to exist. It was a rough, tough, hard life, and sex was very important. It stimulated one group to attack another, to spread the seeds, to increase the population. And, many times, over a few million years, there was a severe risk of the population being eliminated. You were, what you could call, an endangered species, many times, and you survived for a number of reasons. One of these was the success, and pleasure, of sex. But, it is only of benefit if you have a body. There is no pleasure in sex if you do not have a body. There is no purpose in it. Although it appears to be important on the Earth plane, in fact, it has probably been too important, and created numbers that are too great for the size of the planet; in the spirit world it is not important. There are memories, and traces of memories, of the joys of sexual activity in the Earth plane, carried into the spirit world. They are just pleasant memories.

For those going back to the Earth for another life, it can be an important thought; it can help in the decision making, whether to go back as a little baby girl, or a baby boy, and continue to grow until those pleasures return. So, there is some thought amongst those of the levels where a return to Earth is likely, or possible, or beneficial. There is an awareness of masculinity, femininity, and the thoughts of him and her, he and she, continue. When that book was being given to Arthur, it was going to be read by souls in bodies, males and females, who might have an interest in the history of their origins, and that involved the sexes, so they were introduced early in the book, and they were shown to be one of the major causes stimulating the population to take what they could get, to ensure they had sufficient food, sufficient weapons, new weapons, developments which brought other benefits to the population. In those times, men were the more dominant of the two. Women tended to be less muscular, less powerful, but they used their brains and that gift of compassion, which came in very early, to help them, by one way or another, to remain a strong partnership, rather than a weak partnership with the males.

When talking about the committee involved in monitoring the progress of those hominids, and early people, the committee were from my group. None of them were men, or women. They had names. Ywancontin has a similar name to mine, and Arthur has not mastered the pronunciation, yet. He has to breathe in on the middle syllable. But none of that committee were men or women. They were advanced spirits from my group. They are advanced spirits in my group now. We are all moving forward, and we are all aware of the responsibilities of such a group, for reporting human progress, and they know to whom they have to report, to a higher level, as you call it, a more advanced soul, or group of souls with whom we are linked. So, it was easy to refer to them all as 'he', because of the potential readership. If we had called them all 'she', which would be just as wrong as calling them all 'he', that might have deterred some of the more masculine type of people who might read it, but it is immaterial. They have no thoughts, or inclinations, they have only the awareness of our own abilities, or lack of abilities, on the Earth plane at any time. Thank you.

C.   Thank you. Do you have a question, Maria?

M.   You just spoke about the 'she' and the 'him'.   Can you explain to me about how we do overrun, at this time, with homosexuality?

It is an Earth problem, Maria. Those of us who are not involved in the sexuality, in the spirit world, and that means most of us, are sometimes puzzled; and, sometimes we pray to God for enlightenment, but, we do not condemn a female who has masculine tendencies, or the opposite, with a man who feels that he has feminine tendencies.   For those living on the Earth, it can be different; there can be strong feelings, of revulsion, or joy, and of their own nature.   The two sexes, which you read about in the bible, starting with Adam and Eve, were described as a blessing to the humankind, as it was all about to be, was a very strong urge for the creation of new humans.   In those days, we did not think of them as human souls.   It was a defence mechanism for maintaining the strength of the group, growing our own recruits, who would, from an early age, start to help with the collection and preparation of food, to feed the group, the tribe.   It was essential, because the adults did not live very

CHAPTER SIX

long. Many of them died in infancy, and learnt very little. They were of little use to the tribe, unless they were used as food. The need to increase numbers was so essential, that there was this tremendous driving force encouraging the male and female to unite and create more family, more souls, and more life in the tribe. It was an extremely strong urge, and there was annoyance, anger on occasions, when one of the tribe said 'no, I do not wish to mate'. In the early days, another one, another female, who was willing, would soon be found, and relief for the urge was experienced. As these tribes became more settled, and built more permanent homes, in areas like the mouth of a river, or a suitable place for crossing a river, a ford, things changed. The situation changed. There was an increase in philosophising, thinking about life, asking questions, why? And a stronger, dominant, male, who was unable to satisfy his lusts in the normal, usual, way, sometimes looked elsewhere, and unnatural desires were sometimes started, and at times encouraged and enjoyed. That had an immediate reaction from others. So, with a small percentage of the male population, living what was called an unnatural life, tension was created, there was fighting, criticism, death; and it became frowned upon generally. But, that did not stop those unnatural urges, which continue to this day. Now we see homosexuality flaunted on television, openly admitted, and creating more tension, more stress, in the general population, than it did in the past, when all the stress and tension was felt by those who had the unnatural urges. The Romans were famous for encouraging 'freedom of living', as they called it, and that could have been part of the cause of the fall of their empire. There was corruption, and that could be happening now. There are other things happening now, which could lead to much more serious situations in the human race. So, in answer to your question, it cannot be eliminated, because it exists. It is a corruption of God's purpose of having male and female, but each one has the freedom to choose, and if he chooses to be of an unusual inclination, that is his choice, and, as with all other problems, in ethics, the way of life, each individual carries

79

within him, or her, a record, which will be put before him, or her, on their return home, and they can then face and explain, if they wish to.

I do not think we can say much more.

C. Do you want to finish now, Antony?

I do not mind another question.

M. Can I just add to that; we say that he or she is in the wrong body, and the soul chooses the body to be in?

Yes. Yes.

M. Right.   That is what I wanted to know.

They are not happy in that body. They are not in the wrong body. They are unhappy in the body, in which they find themselves.

Let us go back to the time before conception.   We have done this before, but this is all related.   Before a child is born, the soul, that is going to occupy that body, chooses where to go, and that body is going to be either masculine or feminine, almost invariably.   There are exceptions, but almost invariably, they know whether they are going into a boy's embryo, or a girl's.   The decision has been made.   Normally, that would work out well.

But then they say, they find themselves in a body where they are not happy. There is a stage, soon after conception, where the embryo could develop either into a boy or a girl.   That is where some of the problems arise. A little indecision; don't ask me by whom, but, there is a little indecision about the sex of the child, and that can be very distressing to the soul that occupies that body.   It is no fault of their own, but they had intended to have a boy's body, and then they find that it is a girl's, or vice versa. So it is not the fault of the soul concerned in those cases.   There can be cases where a soul, in a boy's body, wishes to experience what it is like to be a girl, or vice versa. They make a conscious decision to think like one of the opposite sex, to wear the clothes, and say they feel happy in the clothes of the other sex. That could be the decision of the soul concerned. They have that freedom, if they wish. They may feel it is such a strong urge that they cannot resist it. And they can become very unhappy people. It is sad. They can become very disillusioned, mentally disturbed, and that can even lead to suicide, in some cases. Very sad. And that suicide is a decision of the soul. So, they have to face that when they return home, face that situation. With such a multiplicity of new bodies, some with new souls, some with old souls, coming to the Earth plane, vast numbers, to the point where the population can be getting its own bad conditions, which will lead to the loss of life, merely through numbers, it is not surprising that, where you have two lines of humans, male and female, some with a few of the attributes of the other, there are complications, there are misconceptions, mistakes, there are errors of judgement in their decision making, that can lead to the unhappiness of a man feeling he is in a woman's body, or a woman feeling she is in a man's body. It is a possibility, and it is also possible that the souls concerned have chosen to be put into that dilemma, as a task, as a problem to be faced. There is always the hope that, if they did so, they will find their way through it. We see effeminate men who are extremely good in management, organisation, control, investigation, philosophy, poetry, music. Many of these people, who are slightly different from the norm, have some wonderful assets. There are many male nurses who are delightful people, clergymen, who only want to help others and are inclined to be effeminate. They can be delightful people, they can follow God's path. It can be a very testing time for them, from the sexual point of view, but they have so much to give, so much compassion in a male nurse, when a masculine man would scoff at it and laugh and say, he is queer, he is odd. But, we need compassion. It was introduced, as you know, to a female, but there are many men who are compassionate, and that can be a good thing. So we must not attempt to judge them. We see them as individual souls who have an opportunity to make their own decisions, and to move forward on their own path, and that is it. Does that help you?

M. Thank you.

P. Antony, before we close, may I say that, when I asked a question before, when I asked, do we choose to come back to the Earth plane, or are we told to? I was speaking to a friend this afternoon, and she said, in the conversation, when I thought of you immediately, she said, 'you know, Phyllis, we are sent down to this Earth plane, we are told how many times we have to come'. I said, I have heard that we choose, and she accepted that. I was really grateful for your information, Antony, and it just gave me joy in my heart.

She felt that she had been told?

It is possible, that some of her guides and helpers in the spirit world have said to her, you know this problem that is troubling you, this block on your progress, this lack of experience of so-and-so? Now, if you went back, and had another life, you could pick a family, where you would be placed in that situation, and you would then find out what the answer to the problem is. And she may have said, 'very good, I like that', chosen the family and come back, and been convinced that she had been told to come back.

P. I see.

It is a question of how they take advice. That decision was hers. The decision to listen to the advice was hers, and the decision to take it was hers. The advice would have been given to her, with the best intention, from someone who had had a similar experience, and was able to inform, to advise, but never to order her back, saying you must go back. Advice can be listened to, but does not have to be taken, unless it is wished.

CHAPTER SIX

P.   I found it very nice to remember some of our conversations. Thank you.

Good.   How is that, Carole?

C.   I think that a lot of questions have been answered.   Arthur has had a bit of a tiring day, today, so I think we could close now, if you don't mind.   Thank you coming, with your helpers, and all your group.

Before I go, can I say to these two ladies, you talk about spirit, 'I believe spirit does this, I believe spirit does that, I must tell spirit.   I would just like you to imagine spirit, in some sort of form of what it is.   Imagine that every spiritual group, and that can be from what you call level two upwards, has an awareness of others; every group has the members linked with each other, to form that group, whatever they call themselves, and those groups are linked with other groups on the same or similar levels.   And then, as you progress, you become aware of other, more advanced groups, as you say, on higher levels.   All of those groups, all similarly linked. The level at which my group operates, has other groups, similarly linked, and we are aware of linkage with all the other groups, all the way down to those who are at the beginning of their path.   We are aware of other groups linking with us from above.   So imagine spirit as that mass of groups, all interlinked, with different responsibilities, as that one entity, spirit.   The power of spirit is enormous.   It is God-given, growing, it can move the planets, and it can move the galaxies. It is enormous.

And that is some of the power of God, who loves you all. Bless you all.

It is good to see you all again, after your enforced break, you look better for it.   Are you ready for more questions, more answers?

C.   Yes, there are only the two of us this week, as Maria is helping out a friend, who has had a tragic event in her life.   She is needed elsewhere this week.   As we are talking about friends, a friend of ours, named Glo, has asked if she could comment on her question.   Would this be allowed, please?

Yes, you give me the question.

C.   My daughter, Angela, is estranged from me, rejecting all my attempts to communicate with her.   Will she ever let me back into her life, so that we can talk and move forward?

And that is from Glo?

C.   Yes, she has multiple sclerosis.   She is a lovely soul, very cheerful, and has had much tragedy in her life, and this is upsetting her very much, at the moment.   She wonders if you could give guidance, or advice to her, as to how to deal with the situation?

Let us all give this some thought.

It is good that the reason for asking the question is the desire to move forward.   That is the whole purpose of our linking, our communication, and the continuing meetings and discussions. I can picture Glo, using Arthur's memory, I can see her, and I feel for her.   Let us all send out our thoughts to her, giving her strength, good wishes from spirit to face the problems, of which she has more than her share.

In answer to the question, it can be simply, yes.   You will meet again. You will be reconciled, but I cannot tell you the place, or the date, where this will take place. That is not information available at this point. So yes, you will be reconciled, but a number of things are needed to take place, in order to bring that about. Firstly, Angela will need to increase her awareness of spiritual values, nearer to the level of her mother. She will need to develop that ingredient, introduced to the human race, so long ago, compassion. She is already aware of her mother's physical condition and problems, and has hardened her heart to the situation. She has become determined to prove that she is totally right, and that her mother is totally wrong. Those extreme conditions rarely apply in any dispute. There is usually an awareness of right and wrong, on both sides of any argument, but she does not accept that, at this moment. So, Glo need not make any further move of self-criticism for lack of progress. There is little that she should be doing, or is able to do, to bring about that change in Angela. We all know that each soul is on a path which leads forward, eventually leads to God, but it is a path strewn with boulders, where it is easy to make a false step, or create damage to oneself and others. That is part of the path on which Angela is walking; when she walks. There are times when she stands still and makes little progress. It is a matter of time before something causes her to move forward. That cause is ahead of her. It cannot be disclosed, but it will happen. She will receive a shock, a jolt, an unpleasant surprise, which will make her open herself to the voice of her spirit guides, who are aware of the problems. They will not miss the opportunity to enlighten her to a number of personal deficiencies, particularly, consideration for others, any others, a feeling of empathy for colleagues, friends, and casual acquaintances, a willingness to smile, to warm to others in a giving way, an awareness of her own mother's personal unhappiness, which has been created by disagreement a long time ago, a disagreement which could be resolved with a little compassion, from each to the other. So, yes, they will be reconciled. We pray for Glo to have the patience, the acceptance of a situation, in order to reduce the stress on herself, physically, mentally, spiritually. She sends out so many kind thoughts, herself, which are received and welcomed. As we have discussed, in this group, on more than one occasion, where a person, a soul in a body, is aware of pain, caused by hate and dislike being aimed at them, from another, the old-fashioned remedies, of revenge, and worse, are not effective. The way forward, in that situation, is to send out loving thoughts, healing, unconditional love, to the person who is so full of hate. Surround them with good wishes, and completely immerse them in white light, which is so effective at removing the darkness of hate, day after day, night after night; sending out those loving thoughts, without any criticism, rancour; only a desire to help. Angela's guides will be fully aware of benefits of receiving that light around the daughter. It is then only a matter of time.

It could be cured without a dramatic shock, a surprise, a physical hurt, mental anguish, or the extreme of bereavement. Those shocks may not be necessary. Glo is fully capable, and fully understands what I have just said. The healing light will be amplified from spirit, through spirit, to the spirit in the body of Angela. She will receive blessings and wonder, why? Her conscience will be tweaked. There will be a surprise, and she will ask why. And once she starts asking the questions, those listening will give her the answer. You have been deliberately unkind to your mother, the soul who gave you birth, who loved you, and will always love you.

Once that sinks in, Angela will be back on the path, moving in the right direction, and wanting to ask for forgiveness, wanting to warm to her mother again, and, for that, she will be blessed by all. Does that answer your question?

C. Yes, thank you. I am sure that will bring her a lot of comfort.

P. Antony, I feel that the daughter is very frightened of something. I don't know the family at all, but, listening to you, I just get that feeling.

CHAPTER SEVEN

That is interesting. Most souls in bodies, who do something wrong, from the extreme of working for the dark forces, to the more normal ones, of which we have all had our share, of selfishness, thinking more of one's ego than the effect that the actions will have on others, show these reactions to a feeling of fear, or they sometimes create a feeling of fear. That is a normal reaction to the awareness of doing something wrong.

C. Can we pass on to something entirely different, now?
You are going to be very pleased with this question, because I am going to talk about level eleven! I know you love the levels, when we refer to them, in that way. You are on level eleven, as we understand. How will you know when you have advanced, enough, to go on to level twelve, and who decides this?

The answer is that I won't know. I will find myself there. I will have been moved, if and when that happens. I say if, but I am optimistic that I will not only make it into level twelve, but that I will move beyond, into the bliss that I have already mentioned. That, if it happens, will occur so subtly, so quietly, that I will feel that I have been standing still and the calendar, on the wall, instead of saying, it is the 11th, will say it is the 12th. It will have changed without my awareness.

C. Does that happen on each level, as we move up?

Yes.

C. You are suddenly aware that you have moved? Who decides?

I will come to the first part, first. You don't move. You find yourself in a different condition, a different state of awareness, and the changes are so small, so refined, that the awareness does not come until quite a long time afterwards. It is not important to note the day or the time. We do not count days and years of promotion.

We just have the joy of an opening of the heart, an opening of the soul, whatever word you like to use. It is an opening to an improved awareness. It is not moving from one level to another. You asked me, in the early days, last year, what level I was on. I had to think of a number, and give you it. I plumped for eleven because it is evenly balanced, two figures; but we do not count in that way now. We do not count levels. The point that I wished to make at that time, and now, is that I have made progress. I don't boast about it. I don't say how wonderful it is, because that would tend to put me down to level 'one', not 'one one'.

The ego, which I would be showing, if I had boasted about the number eleven, the ego, is one of the biggest barriers to progress from any stage to the next one. You will see it. I have seen it. I have experienced it. The ego; me, me, me. I have heard that expression on your lips, about someone else. And then, judgement comes into it, as well, which is another form of ego. I am better than that; ego!

Humility is the opposite of ego. The humble one makes more progress than the egotist. So, you might worry about what is the number of my level. That is a problem that you will overcome. You will learn to accept that, if you are on a more advanced stage of awareness than another soul, that is merely because you have learned more than that other soul, who is also learning, and who could move forward quicker than you are moving forward, and become of a higher level, as you call them, than you. That happens. Some souls leapfrog ahead of others. Some slip back. Some stand still. It is a continual movement forward, whether it is a movement forward at zero speed, or at a greater speed; at any speed. We do not measure speed. We do not like to measure levels, but you know that now?

C. I like levels. I can relate to it. I can see it better. I can understand it better.

That is the Earthly eagerness to measure. You have miles, you have yards, you have feet, kilometres; endless different ways of measuring. And, where does it get you? It gets you exactly where you are. There is no need to measure.

You asked another question. Who decides when a soul should move to a higher level? It could be the soul, himself, or herself. It might not be, though. Throughout spirit, which, as you know, is the sum total of all the linked souls, linked groups of souls, throughout the universe, there is an awareness of the condition, the state, the education, the knowledge, the measurement, (if you want to measure), their humility, their compassion, their love, their unconditional love for others, if that is all measured, (it is difficult to imagine), but, there is an awareness of that condition, for each soul, throughout spirit. And that soul knows where it stands. That is all there is to it. The soul knows it must learn, it must advance in all spiritual matters, in order to make progress.

C. Would all your group go forward together, or would that be the individuals going forward, the individual member of the group?

You mean, would one member of our group break away and find themselves on another level? Is that what you mean?

C. Yes, and would one soul from a lower group be able to work to get into your group?

The advancement of one soul does not open an opportunity for promotion of another soul on a lower level. Those are human, Earthly, thoughts. When I say that I am a member of a group, all linked with one another, my group brothers, I call them, (they could be called group sisters, group things; whatever word you use), we have worked together for a long time, we have advanced for a long time. The advancement of each spirit, in that group, helps the others. The awareness, of opportunities for advancement in one, gives that same awareness to each member of the group. So a group, working together, thinking together, sharing thoughts, sharing desires for advancement, is likely to find that the group is suddenly aware, or has suddenly gained the knowledge of something else, some new aspect, an aspect of an attitude to life that they had not had before. They had not moved. They are still sat in their castle, or whatever you call it. They have not moved, but they have this greater awareness. So, in Earthly thinking, they have moved. They have advanced, and, if anyone asked them, at what level were they, then, and they had to think of a number, they might say seven, or twelve, because the numbers do not mean anything. But, they have advanced. That is all there is to it. All that is important is that they have advanced. They have increased their awareness of some fascinating aspect of life. They have a new view of the Creator. They have a new way of helping others, who are less advanced. So here I am trying to use your language, your mathematics, to explain something from God. I have my limitations, your language has its limitations, but I am trying to help you to have the right attitude to spirit, rather than having an obsession with spirit levels, which are used in carpentry, I believe?

C. Yes, it is because we are in a physical body, and the knowledge we have gained from spirit guides, who have come through, lectures that we have attended, dealing with colour healing, etc., we had a guide come through, and he was talking about the levels, and he showed us a diagram of levels. He was trying to explain the levels, and how many there were, and he said he was on level eleven, you see. This is why we can refer to the higher awareness, looking at it in that sense, you understand?

He was wanting to help you. I can see his chart, now, in Arthur's memory. I can see it there. I can see him trying to explain to you, a universe, in front of you, with another at the front and the back of you, another at each side of you, and another at each side of those, and above and below them, an infinite number of universes, he called them. There are a similar number of levels, if only you could measure them, but, you cannot. There is not a method of measuring levels of awareness.

CHAPTER SEVEN

C. That is the way that we could understand, at that time.

Yes, and it made you think. You have carried that, and Arthur has carried that in his memory; but that is not the full picture.

C. Yes, I am aware of that now.

His name was given as John, I think? John wished to help you. He had promised to help you with an understanding of spiritual levels of advancement, and he kept his promise. There were charts, and maps, and rulers, and multiplication tables. He was able to confuse you more, and I wish to reduce that confusion, by telling you, do not worry about levels, only have an eagerness to make progress, to advance your own progress, and to help all your friends and loved ones to make progress. That is the message. That is the answer to all the problems in the world, in the universe, today.

C. Thank you. Do you want another question?

Do you have another question?

C. I think Phyllis has a question.

P. Well, I haven't got a question, Antony. It is just an observation, if I may speak to you about it.

If we can turn it into a question, we will do.

P. When reading the book, The Path, I was so absolutely fascinated by how the beings gradually become psychic, and they developed spiritual senses, and, even to this day, when one talks to some people, they think you are not quite normal if you speak of spiritual things. I suppose it is because they don't have the same understanding that we are privileged to have here today. So, do you think that some things never change, or that some people are not quite ready to understand, or accept?

You have made that into quite a few questions. I understand what you are meaning. You asked, firstly, a simple question. Are some people not yet ready to understand?

They think that they are not. They decide that they are not ready to understand. They close their minds to a spiritual thought, but, each one of those questioned has a spirit guide, has helpers who have been with them all the time, waiting for the opportunity to encourage them to look at the path, get on the path, and move forward. But, they are not ready for that, because they are held back by some of the barriers to progress. I mentioned one earlier, the ego, the person who knows everything. They know the answer to every problem. They know that they are right, and everyone who disagrees with them is wrong.

There was a mention earlier, about Glo and her daughter. There is a touch of the ego there; the knowledge that you are right and everyone else is utterly wrong. And that is difficult to progress from.

You mentioned some of the psychic abilities of some of the early people. One of the psychic abilities was the ability to read another's mind; to use telepathy to communicate. That was, in the early days, the only method. And you see that still, today, demonstrated when a shoal of fish change direction, ninety degrees, instantly. That is not done by them calling; let's turn left, boys and girls, and them hearing it and deciding to obey. That is telepathic communication, a sudden switch, and away.

P. It's like the birds flying.

Yes, like the starlings and the rooks, masses of birds, changing direction, so that they don't hit each other. That is telepathy. That is what most creatures used in their early days of nature. It was only the introduction of language, which developed from grunts, and nods, and shouts from one hominid to another, that did away with the need for telepathy, or, it reduced its usage. And so, the ability to communicate, mentally, has faded, but not faded completely. Two people, living together, over a period of time, both think the same thing at the same time. That is telepathy. That is proof. But, the ability is still there; the latent ability to send a thought to another without making any noise, but the ability to rely on it, and know it will work, is much less than the apparent usage of it. But it works. That was an early form of communication, and, at the same time, there was an awareness of souls without bodies; spirit, moving amongst them. If you remember, there was one female who saw one of the 'tall ones'? She was frightened to death, poor creature. The 'tall ones', yes, they all remember it. They were surprised, and it shows how imperfect the near-perfect ones are. They did not plan ahead, and they created chaos, havoc, for those tree-dwellers, who fell off the branches. That was another thing to learn, another experience that they had not had before in spirit, and they are still aware of that.

P.   It fascinated me, Antony, when the beings started to cover their bodies for warmth.   As I walk through the shops, now, and I think how things have progressed, and how we take it all, so much for granted, that we go in and ask the assistant that we would like that garment.   When you think back, it gives you the most wonderful feeling to think how it all started, well, it does for me anyway.

When they were starting to move about Africa, the climate there was only slightly warmer than it is there now, and they did not need many clothes, they did not need cover, until they started climbing the mountains, driven there by the great beasts that wished to devour them. So, when they had the opportunity to kill the great beasts, they cut the fur off, (the pelts), and were eventually able to make clothing out of it and keep themselves warm.

In that way, they were able to spread to the temperate parts of the world, and on to the colder parts.

P.   They were able to beat the leather and make it soft, more comfortable.

They were a long time finding what chemical to apply when they beat the leather, but, they found it.

P. I found it very fascinating to read the book. Thank you very much.

Good. Thank you for your observation.

C. I would like to ask about the spirit body, or the spirit, if you like. We are told that, sometimes, the spirit needs to rest. Is this true? When we pass over, very often, we are told, if it has been a traumatic passing, the spirit needs to rest?

Some spirits, in a body, have difficult final stages of life on Earth, a final testing period. If they live to a ripe old age, they tend to get more pain and discomfort as the body wears out, and that is all part of the process of learning, adaptation, and readying for transition. After many months, or even years, of such discomfort, they can feel completely exhausted, to the point of being relieved when the soul leaves the body, but it still has a residual effect on the soul. It is at the end of an exhausting period, and the relief from pain, at the time of transition, is wonderful. The memory of it continues, with the shock of finding oneself in a totally new environment. If they have not been spiritually inclined beforehand, it is a shock. For those with your experience, and others in your movement, it is not a shock at all; it is just a great joy. It is something to be welcomed, when it happens; and you find that you must go back immediately, to check on the poor souls who have been shocked by your death, by the bereavement; you want to comfort them. You particularly want to go when they meet at, or just after, the funeral. You are fascinated. You want to dance at your funeral; as you know, you have seen them. Arthur has seen them dancing at their funeral, amongst the spirits who are there. It is a joyful time, and it is not easy to communicate, immediately. Some clergy, some priests, do their best to try to comfort those who are left behind, those who may have no idea of what has happened, and, afterwards, can feel utterly shocked at having been left behind, with a reduced number in the family, and all the problems that arise, financial problems, bickering over funeral wishes, the will. They have a lot to worry about, and they do enjoy that worry. It seems to be natural, when there should be joy. You have heard the expression, 'it was a relief, really', and that can be very true when a loved one, in pain, is taken away, it can be a great relief for the loved one. The unselfish person might send them a kind and loving thought and wish them well, with blessings. Those who are untrained in spiritual ways have mixed-up feelings, at those times. They sob their hearts out; they have been deprived of their loved ones, their source of income, and their source of strength, friendship. It is one of the blessings that you, and others like you, can pass on to those who are bereaved, and give them comfort, by spending some time with them, as Maria is doing tonight. It is a good thing, to do that.

Sooner or later, the bereaved one will realise what a blessing it was to have a friend at that time, and start asking questions, start wondering, listening to that inner voice which explains it to her, if she listens. Now, have I missed any part of your question?

C. No. The reason I asked that, going back now to John. He uses a friend to do psychic surgery, and he works through him. He once said to me that he spends more time on the Earth plane than he does in spirit, because he is working through Brian so much, that most of his time is spent here, doing this important work. He once told me that he must go back, because he was feeling heavy, and he needed to be cleansed. That was one of the points I was going to ask you about. The other was about whether spirit needed to rest. Although there is no physical body any more to worry about, surely, the thoughts on the Earth plane, that go out to that spirit that took their transition, must be picked up and felt by that spirit?

Yes, there is a residue of exhaustion, particularly if it has been a traumatic last few days or weeks for them. That feeling of exhaustion would be carried forward as a desire for rest. As for feeling heavy, on the Earth plane, I think that you might be getting the message that he has been working in a heavy body, working through the Earthly healer, Brian. Working in that body, for only short periods; most of the time he is accompanying that body which is doing physical work, massage, manipulation; that could give him a feeling of heaviness, working in that body, the residue of thought, rather than the actual weight. He is not aware of weight, he is aware of the (I was going to say lethargy) the slowness of working in a tired old body, as he is, with a bad heart. He is aware of that, and he calls it (I haven't quite got the name) it is a feeling of having to push the body, and that is working and affecting the heart. It is tiring a tired old heart, as you know.

C. Yes, I think it is because it is so quick in spirit, isn't it?

You say, 'quick'. We are back in the business of measuring speed.

C. Vibration is the word that I want.

Yes, that could be more the meaning of it. If you are in spirit in London, and you want to be in New York, you are there. That isn't speed; that is instant. You cannot measure the speed of movement. You are there. You are where you want to be, because you have nothing physical to move.

C. Do you not have to lower your vibrations to come into our heavy atmosphere?

We don't measure. We try to get away from measuring, and distance, and weight. We might describe the atmosphere as heavy. Some people talk of heavy vibrations, lower vibrations, slower vibrations; vibrations of what? There is nothing physical in spirit, so what can be vibrating?

CHAPTER SEVEN

C. But, we are going at a slower rate here, aren't we?

Very much slower.

C. That's what I'm trying to say.

But, what is going where, at this slower rate?

C. We understand that, when guides come to use us, on the Earth plane, they lower their vibrations to come into our Earthly atmosphere.

Oh, yes, I understand what you are meaning now. When moving into a physical body, on this Earth plane, everything seems a 'plod', slow, much slower. Yes, you are calling that 'slower vibrations'. Yes, everything is much slower. If you want to move from A to B, you start moving from A, in the direction of B, eventually, you get to B and then you stop, and you are there. But, in spirit, if you want to go to A or B, you are there, in both of them, if you want, instantly. It is difficult to compare. You shouldn't try to compare. The awareness of tiredness, when working in human bodies, is the awareness of the tiredness of the human body, not of the spirit.

C. Yes, that was what I wanted to clarify.

It is a spiritual awareness of the slowness, the weight, of which we don't want to know, but it is thrust upon us when we are working inside a human body.

C. But, you will understand, Antony, these are the sort of questions that are put to us, at services and in group work.

This is another question. If you are having difficult questions to answer, what I would call 'tricky questions', I would, first of all ask, why is that question being asked? When I find that out, by being told, which I am; it helps with the answer. So, when you are asked a question about the vibrations, the speed of vibrations, by some clever person in the congregation, who wants to trap you, it is always a good thing to start off with, 'that's a very interesting question, why do you want to know?' Eventually, you find that they just wanted to trap you, when they admit that they wanted to see if you gave the same answer as somebody else had given them. They cannot conceal the truth from you, if you ask them the right questions.

Those who are wanting to trap you are troublemakers, are 'clever-dickies', 'clever-clogs', but they are trying to appear to be clever, in front of an audience, a congregation, and at your cost. This is one good reason for asking for protection before you start, 'Deliver us from evil'. If the intentions of that questioner are evil, they won't even be able to ask the question. If the intentions are merely to embarrass you, that is unkind, destructive, and not worth pursuing. If you are asked a question about rates of vibration, speed of this, and the distance of that, you can say, simply, I can tell you something about the spirit world, which will answer all those questions. They are not involved in speed, or distance, or age, or level numbers. Those are all Earthly matters, now, next question, please.

C.   I always say that I can only answer questions which are on my own level of understanding.

Good, yes.

C.   In that way, if I can't answer the question truthfully, then I just can't, so they have to ask somebody with more knowledge than me.

There are questions you might ask that I can't answer.

C.   I don't think so.

CHAPTER SEVEN

Because I am not allowed, by spiritual law. I cannot give you the date of Glo's reconciliation with Angela. It is not right. I cannot give you the date or time of your transition.

C. I would like to know.

You would not! It is far better for you to continue on your productive path forward.

C. I think that when you are not very well, and things are looking a bit black, it is very hard to be positive. I have felt, lately, that I have lost confidence, and in my spiritual work, I will never do another service again. It went to that stage, and I thought, I have been here before.

That was why you were made to rest. That was why I did not come back to hold a group meeting, like this, with you, for a matter of four or five weeks.

C. Hopefully, we will go forward now, and do a little more work.

I hope so. Have you any more questions?

P. No. I just want to thank you, Antony, for answering and coming to my help when I felt so low. Thank you very much.

You all needed a rest. You can put too much physical effort into spiritual work, and you pay the price.

C. We do thank you for coming. Hopefully, we can meet again next week. Bless you.

Good evening. A little below par, today? Not I, but one or two of you.

C. Will you be alright, working with Arthur?

I will try to keep him under control, but it is not easy. But do not worry. He will not cough when I am talking.

C. He has been told not to, so, shall we start with the questions?

Do you have questions for me?

C. Yes, I do have one. It is from a personal experience I went through, some time ago, which might be helpful to other people, when they read the manuscript. It is to do with out of body experiences. Now, I was receiving healing, at one time. It is rather unusual for me to have such an experience, whilst receiving healing. The next moment, I was in the corner of the room, looking down on my body. As I watched, a young Indian squaw came out of my body, with her arms outstretched. To me, it was a sign, asking for deliverance. Once I recognised this, I was back in my body again. I wonder if you could enlighten me on this, and explain why that happened, and what was the purpose of my seeing this young Indian girl?

Yes. It is good to hear this. It was a beautiful experience for you; and for her. She was a spirit, without a body, and she was able to visit you, in the way that she did. You, at the time, became a spirit without a body, because you were without yours, but the link was not broken. You retained your link with the Earth plane. The purpose, of you both having that experience, arose from a mutual

100

agreement, mutual consent, that you had each worked together, spiritually. She had, for a time, been one of your guides. She was aware of your condition, and she was aware that you were receiving healing, which she experienced, by taking up your body space. It was good for her to gain a greater knowledge, a greater awareness, of you as a spirit with a body. She, by her presence, helped with the healing that you were receiving at that time. She wished for you to be aware of her appearance, as well as presence, and you have retained that in your memory, with joy and love, ever since, and it will remain with you.

If that was the first time, that you remember, of your spirit being temporarily detached from your body, it was not the first time. You have had previous experiences in childhood, and as you were growing into an adult, and it passed so quickly that you felt it was a daydream, a thought, but, it has happened before, and it could happen again. The experience is pleasant, joyful. You have no feeling of fear, as you look down on your body, and even, when eventually you come to the time of transition, you will feel the same. Because of your previous experiences, those you remember, and those that you have forgotten, you will feel very comfortable, and that is all part of the joy of returning home. So there is no need to have any anxiety about any out of body experience.

C. Thank you very much. That is quite right, because I have often thought about it, and she is a very pretty young girl. I also have a psychic drawing of her, so I knew she was the helper that I had seen in the picture that had been given to me. I thought I would ask that because I had another experience, years ago, that is still remembered, but it was not to do with healing. It was not exactly like that. I was talking to a gentleman at the time, and I felt that he was still on the Earth plane, Earth bound. He needed help to get away. It leads me up to the next question of rescue work, and I have had many experiences of this.

We were talking of groups last week, and I believe that I belong to the White Rose group, which helps people who are in the darkness, what we call rescue work. Is this so?

That is so.

C. I remember, sometimes, where I have been, and other times, I don't, but, that out of the body experience was a pleasure, and one that I will never forget. Many people have these experiences, I know; probably in different ways, and some mean more to them than others, but that particular occasion, when I was in a pretty low state myself, was a wonderful thing to experience.

Could you tell me, please, if there will ever be a second coming of Christ?

Your are asking me to tell you God's will? I have been trying to do that, in my many meetings with you, in this group, but it is only possible to tell you part of God's will. Some parts, he does not divulge to us.

C. Why I asked that is because there is something mentioned in the Bible; something about the state of the Earth plane or I have heard of it or read of it somewhere. I wondered if that was fiction, really, or whether there was any truth in it at all?

Let me tell you what I may tell you.

The first coming had more impact on the human population of this planet than the birth of any other human being. We have talked of it before. It is accepted, in your measurement of time in the date, and in countries claiming to be Christian, but, who live a heathen way of life. There are many, who have been so impressed with the stories of his life, that are printed, they were so impressed that they came to the conclusion, probably very quickly, that it must have been a wonderful time to be on the Earth throughout his life, and afterwards, when, despite his followers being persecuted, they were not eliminated. Their followers can be counted in their multimillions now. So, with all that awareness of the joys he brought, and left behind, it is a natural, human, thought; wouldn't it be wonderful if he came again? When he came the first time, he was taken to the top of a high mountain and shown most of the civilised world, in those parts, and he was offered control, by temptation. He refused the temptation, then; and I think you might agree that, if he was offered the opportunity to put the world to rights, on a second visit, he might, again, decline the offer. The idea of him coming again raises the question, would he be recognised by all those who do not believe in him? It also raises the question about belief in his continued existence. You know that your spirit lives forever: so you know that his spirit lives forever, and the majority of spirits in the spirit world, in what you call heaven, spend much of their time considering the problems on the Earth plane. I think you will agree that he is still here.

So, are you referring to him taking on a body again, being born again, as a child? You are? That is a different question. Have no doubt that he is still around, as many of his followers are, and continue to be. So, if your question is, will he come again and be born again as a child, and introduce himself to his existing believers, and non-believers, that is a question. In his first coming, his mother was a pure virgin. You will agree that there will be difficulty in finding one today? Without making fun of the situation, there is no doubt that one would be found. The decision, whether he comes again, or continues to stay with us, is with him and his Father-God. And there it will remain.

P. Antony, it concerns me, or worries me quite a bit, that there is so much violence in the world, and it seems to grow. One gets a little frightened these days. Do you think that the violence will increase, or decrease?

How do you measure violence?

P. Well, people taking other people's lives, stabbing, or, when you watch the television, you see things. There seems so much hurt in the world; it seems to be more than in my childhood.

Firstly, if you are worried about these conditions, it does not help you, or them, or their victims, to worry. You have raised a similar question before, and there have been similar questions from others in the group. This world has been described by others, even outside the group, as the 'pits', the lowest depth to which beings can sink. That is an extreme view, because there is no hope in it. From the beginning of time, with humans on the Earth plane, they have been involved in violence. It was part of their nature, which helped them to survive. They were able to be violent to the potential meals, when they met them, whether they were other humans or animals. Violence gave them food. Violence kept them alive. So, there has always been violence; but you are thinking of violence, just for the sake and the pleasure of it?

That developed millions of years ago, also. The successful ones, the strongest enjoyed their strength and violence, and used it to prove their ability. That was an example of ego at its worst. The strong muscular man, who had developed a weapon, with which he could kill more easily than before, more easily than the opponent could kill him, was doing it for pleasure. They call it 'job satisfaction' today. Things are not getting better, obviously; but, things are not getting worse, obviously. It is a continual process. If you were in the field of battle, you would see appalling scenes of violence. There are battles going on today, now.

P. But, people do not have to kill to get a meal these days, Antony?

Sometimes they have to do it to get an oil well, or the bank deposits, or whatever. They may do it to get that position of power; they don't do it just for a meal. They use the same technique just to get their own way. The ego must win. They are always right. There is no immediate hope of all physical violence stopping. It will not stop. It will continue. There are other things ahead of the human race that will give them that trauma to make them ask why? Once they ask why? The inner voice will tell them why, and it will tell them how to avoid it. Until they ask why, they won't be told. They won't listen, if they are told. When I tell you that in the millions of people on the Earth plane, today, all souls in bodies, some are old souls, some are new souls. The new souls may be here for the first time, and they have no residual awareness of right and wrong. You know that they are not supposed to carry it forward, from being a spirit, into the baby's body in which they are born, but, those of you who have been here before, and you all have, do carry a basic inner knowledge somehow, (I don't want to explain it now), but you carry that forward, ask the right questions, get the right answers, and have that awareness of right and wrong.

New souls do not have that, so they have to learn that, if they kill someone, they might be killed, or, if they hit somebody, they might be hit back. And, the only way to learn is to do it. So some of the fighting and warfare, of which you complain, is created by new souls who are in 'basic training', if you want the word, and the older souls could see it. They know it is wrong, they say so, and, depending on whether they can defend themselves, or whether they are far enough apart from the aggressive new souls, they might survive.

P. Thank you. I saw a television programme, that I told Carole and Arthur about, where the creatures in the documentary were similar to the ones in the book that Arthur wrote. What made me smile, and warmed my heart, was the fact that the females in the group would not let the males have any violence, so, of course, I was pleased about that.

I picked that up in Arthur's memory; I can see them. Yes, the interesting thing is that those delightful creatures, I think they called them monkeys, had ancestors who were very similar, five million years ago, and they have not made much progress, because they have found a balance. Unfortunately, there are others, of the human kind, who have used them for meat, and it was thought that they were to be eliminated, which could still happen. Yes, that had links with the story, and it was uncannily similar. I can see them. Thank you.

C. I have a question now, from Arthur.
Having listened to you, over a period of time, I have the impression that you have existed, as a spirit, for longer than there have been human beings on the Earth. Have you ever lived on another planet?

I can give him the answer, and he can log it, can't he?
When I first came to you, the purpose was to communicate with you, and, for that purpose, we developed, over a period of time, this easy linking, using Arthur's mind, and using his words. That has been made easier with practice, but, at the time, I said that my purpose was to help you to make progress spiritually, to help to develop your awareness, to help you to practise thinking, in what you might call a 'heavenly way', thinking of spiritual progress on your own path, to give you an outlook of how things have been happening at our side of the 'divide', if you call it that, and that has been fairly successful.

When I have finished answering this question, I will have one for you!

You ask if I have ever lived on another planet. I can give you an answer to that, now. Yes, frequently. You will be able to, when you return home. You will be able to visit, and live on other planets, see how they have developed, see the similarities and the differences between those planets with similar, but slightly varied atmospheres; with similar, but slightly varied inhabitants, but all God's creatures. That is the point to remember, all created, and given life force, by that spark of love from God; the soul, as you have, and as they have.

Some of these souls have been in existence for many millions of years, many millions, before there was human life on this Earth. So, they did not exist here, in the early days. It is likely, and very probable, that they have experienced life on this planet, in a human body, and they are that much wiser, and more experienced, for it. You, with your knowledge of time, must know that, if you go one hundred million years back, they would not have had much opportunity on this planet, but there are other planets, some of which do not exist, now, whereas, at that time, which is not very far back, in this eternity, we talk about, not very far back, they existed, they had a population of bodies with souls, going through the same sort of experiences, that you do, that you have, and making progress on their path, which continues; if they have not reached the ultimate bliss of which you are aware. So, if you ask me the question, have I come from another planet, that can have an implication that I have no knowledge of this one, but, I can assure you that I have; I have an awareness of a number of other planets, as you may well have, in your basic memory, which is stored here, not with you.

So, I may have met you on another planet, at another time, or I may not, but you may have been there. You may have been on a different other planet. You are not locked into the Earth plane forever. You have had a few lives here. When you check, you may find that you have had a few lives there. So, is that news to you? Does it worry you?

C. It doesn't worry me. It's because, when we put on our televisions, and see the science fiction films, which seem unbelievable and yet, to me, they seem very possible. They are now reaching out more into the galaxies, with our rockets, and so forth, trying to find out if there was ever life on Mars, or other planets, and it seems to be going this way. We often hear of ufo's landing on the Earth plane, space ships, people having encountered entities from these space ships, but, of course, many don't believe them. I feel that this is going on all the time, and people can't accept it. They don't believe it. It is the same with spiritualism and life after death. They cannot believe that you can survive the grave. I can't see why they can't believe it. They want proof, definite proof. This is what we are bombarded with. This is why people get so confused. I accept that there can be higher intelligences than us on other galaxies. Probably, this is why Arthur has asked that other question tonight, because of your higher intelligence and awareness.

You mentioned television programmes; those are created by men, for entertainment. Do you agree with that? But, in doing so, what they call science fiction, is scouring our memories for possible stories, which will be new; the novelty of which will encourage people to pay to watch these films, but, invariably, there is a touch of truth in most of them, almost all of them. I think that if you watch any science fiction, any murder mystery, any tales of the future, you have that feeling, within you, that there is something in that story. It makes good entertainment. It is interesting. It intrigues you. And, I can tell you, there is likely to be some truth in the story.

So, it is interesting to someone who has doubted. There are people who will believe in those stories of space travel, but who will not believe in Jesus Christ. I don't know why they should do that, but, at least, they believe there is a possibility of truth in something that they have not actually experienced other that as a film or as a story. They have some awareness of possibilities, which is a good thing. So, enjoy the stories, enjoy the novelty, the intriguing aspects of other planets are rarely worse than those of the occupants of the Earth plane. They are similar, with their own testing periods of history, their own problems of strife, and learning from it, their own record of their own progress on their own path; which they have to face when it is time to part company with their own body. You can imagine it all happening, so far away that they are unable to visit, or near enough, but still a long way away, that they are able to send a space ship, (which you might call a ufo), which might or might not be in the imagination. They might be so close, but in another dimension. There are many ways in which these things can be pictured in the imagination.

As your brains continue to absorb knowledge, the process will help you to understand that everyone had problems. Everyone has the opportunity to learn from those problems, and from cure of those problems. I wonder why he asked the question?

C. I don't know.

I've got it. Yes, he has worked it out that, if Ywancontin and others, including myself, were all at this stage of advancement, or near it, five million years ago, in the early days of the human population, I must have come from another planet. He was measuring.

C. He is very good at mathematics.

He was counting the years and he had worked out, what he called, a logical conclusion, and there is truth in it. But, we will not go into those details.

Now, it is time for me to ask you a question, the two of you who can answer, each one of you.

This is the eighth time that I have visited you as a group. My intentions were declared. I have not carried them out, completely, but I have wished that you could both learn to see things in a slightly different way, a slightly more advanced way, than you have done in the past. I would like you each to say, in turn, whether you feel you have made that progress, that move in the right direction, and what the result of that progress, if any, has been. Will you say, Carole?

C. Well, to me it has been very helpful, and I know that I am very different, in myself, before you started to come. I thought I knew the answers to lots of spiritual questions. My eyes have been really opened, because I have, as you put it, got another slant on a lot of things appertaining to spirit and spiritual life. I am sure that my awareness has grown, if only a little, and I am sure that I must have progressed a little. I am sure that I must have done. I feel that I have. Without your coming, and helping us with these questions, which I am sure you must have felt were very silly, at times, but they are questions that are relevant at this time in our lives. I feel so grateful, really, I don't know quite how to put it to you, but I am so grateful that you have taken this time, and worked with Arthur, to come through Arthur, to answer these questions and bring us this advanced knowledge. It is all being recorded, and written down; there is a lot for us to absorb and to learn and take in at one time. That is why we are able to play these tapes back, and read from the book that Arthur is compiling at this time, not only to help us, but also to help other people that we are coming in contact with. I see also that, by doing these spiritual services, which we shall do this year, when we finish, but, up to that point, we will help a lot more people, because of the different slant that we now have on certain aspects of spirit. I hope that you feel it has not been a waste of time for you. I'm sure it has not been, or you would not even have attempted to do this. I am sorry that we have not had a bigger group, but it does seem that it has been Phyllis and myself, sometimes there has been Maria, who hopes to come back next week. I feel that what we have learned, and what you have tried to teach us, will be very beneficial in many ways. So, we bless you for that, Antony, and thank you so much.

Thank you. Before Phyllis gives her comments, let me take one or two points. None of you questions have been other than a desire for an answer, so do not think that those questions are criticised. It could have been possible to ask much more basic questions, but you had already passed that stage of awareness. All your questions were welcome and gave an opportunity for being answered. The question of time? I have all the time in eternity, so I do not begrudge one minute, or one hour, of the time that I have spent with you. It has been satisfying, good, and will continue, if you wish, so, thank you for your answer. Now, Phyllis, are you going to make an observation?

P. Well, Antony, I really feel very humble to be in this group, and for you to come to us every week, and I am very, very, grateful, and I feel that I have moved quite a bit, in my understanding, emotionally, and I do approach things differently in my mind, now. For that I am very pleased, thank you very much.

Thank you. You mentioned humility, and I have mentioned it. I can tell you that, the more one advances, the more one needs humility. Humility does not help very much on level one, or level one minus. It is into those dark depths, that Carole, and other helpers, spend their nights, seeking out lost souls, and trying to nudge them into one point five or two, or however you measure it. It is wonderful work. They will all need to be moved on. That is why it takes so long, in eternity, with all those souls making no progress, wallowing in indecisions and negativity. They all need to be urged, stimulated, encouraged, to move upwards, forward. So, those who spend their sleeping hours, as a soul seeking the lost ones, are doing wonderful work, and they will get another flower in their garden each time.

C. Can I just ask you a question, Antony? It came to me while you were talking. I used to really enjoy going into church. When I was feeling upset I used to look forward to going into church, knowing it would make me feel better. It is not very often, now, when I go into a spiritualist church, even when we do a service, that I am very happy about it. I don't feel uplifted when I come out. Is this because of these meetings, because we have moved on? The service does not seem to be so spiritual any more.

Shall I answer that?
There are a number of things which can affect the atmosphere in a church, by atmosphere, I mean spiritual awareness. Some are good. Some are bad. So, let's deal with the bad ones first. As you make progress on your path, and you have, and you are doing, and you will continue to do so, that is, increase awareness, and that awareness will give you the opportunity to have a quick assessment of each soul that you meet, the colour of their aura, the smile on their face, or lack of it, the insincerity, the ignorance.

You will see it all, instantly, and this is where a very fine line needs to be drawn, between awareness of others' shortcomings, and judgement of them. It is not easy to find the difference between those two. It is good. It is right, and it is natural to have an awareness of others' shortcomings, but, if there is the slightest trace of ego that quickly becomes judgement. You will know it. You will be aware of it if it starts. Part of the benefit of your making progress is that you are able to control that sense of judgement, because the only judge of a soul is the soul itself. They can judge themselves. You should not. But, that does not mean to say that you must not recognise any feeling of apprehension, awareness, unhappiness, with another happy soul, who is showing signs of all the basic human vanities. You know them, ego, greed, selfishness; it all comes back to the same thing. You recognise it in the nature of the people you meet in a church, and that is the last place that it should be, isn't it? They should not be like that. You know they should not be like that. So, what can you do about it?

Firstly, recognise it for what it is. It is an awareness of negativity in others. It is not judgement. Keep away from judgement. It is an awareness of their condition. And you, I can see in your mind, you have that awareness about people who are running that church service, the way they do it, the way they chair the service, the way they butt in, when the medium is talking with the voice of another spirit; they butt in, they interrupt. It is sad; recognise it for what it is. It is not judgement of them, but an understanding that they are not in control of themselves. They are not, for want of another expression, they are not advanced sufficiently to be where they are. That is, probably, the most likely reason for you to have feelings of dissatisfaction, the lack of inspiration. You come away from a service feeling worse than when you went in, and you wish that you had not been there? I have got that from Arthur's memory. It is sad, but it is not judgement. It is awareness, and the more advanced you become, and you are becoming more advanced, the more you will recognise that. It is written all over them, whether you see the colour of their aura, or the fact that their mouths are down, their mind is insincere; all are ways of recognising negativity, which is one of the biggest bars to progress. The times you have heard the expression, be positive! Live for today! Look on the good side! There are times when you have to recognise the failure, of others, to be positive.

So, one of our old friends, the white light, is probably the best answer. When you are going into a church, ask for protection, five or six times; smother the place in white light, go in with a smile, knowing that it will help others who see it, and you will feel better when you come out, possibly! Not guaranteed!

C. I think it is because I have always been like this, from the moment that I started working. I want to give of my best. I want spirit to be able to work well through me, to help these people that are sitting there, that have all got problems. Quite a lot are of the younger generation, too, and yet, sometimes, it seems such hard work; there seems to be such a block, they won't give of themselves, and yet they expect everything. I feel more uplifted with these get-togethers, circle work, or philosophy groups at home. I find that I am happier, more uplifted with these sorts of groups, than doing the church work, now. At one time, I loved doing it, but now, I am not so happy with it. I won't say that all services are like it. We have been to places where it has been lovely, and people have been very kind, and it has been a happy service, but, lately, I have not felt like that.

Your next service, when is it?

C. Sunday.

Let me say that a little reassurance can be helpful. It should not be necessary, but, I can assure you that there are many thousands of souls who have benefited from your mediumship, thousands, many thousands, so you are not doing anything wrong. You are doing something extremely good, very beneficial to those in the church. I have heard you say, if I was able to help only one or two people at that service, it was worth going. That is more than true, because you have helped more than the one or two that you think you have helped. If you have any failing at all, it is in the ability to assess your own skills. They are way ahead of your assessment, so how many times do you need to be told that? Relax; you are doing work which is so good. In this service on Sunday, you will be giving clairvoyance after Arthur has given the philosophy? We will change all that! He will not be giving the philosophy; I will!

P.   That will be good.   I will be listening.

You will be there, Phyllis?

P.   I will.

You will recognise it? Saying, good old Antony! 'He said he would be coming, and I know he is there.' And, Arthur will have a rest, (poor Arthur). Now, Phyllis.

P.   I do understand what Carole says, but on some days of the week, some people come into the church, and they just come to hear or try to wait for a message, and then they disappear. They don't come to the church for being in the church. Sunday seems to be a different service altogether, because people come, if you can understand what I mean, to the church for the service, and also, it is a bonus, or a lovely feeling people get, if they receive a message, some people come in very quickly, sit down, and as soon as the service is over, they are out of the doors, and that isn't, to me, coming to the church. I do have understanding, what Carole has said.

When you say they disappear, is that literal?

P.   Yes, they go out of the door very quickly.

CHAPTER EIGHT

Immediately they have had a message?

P.   No, immediately the service is over.

I know one or two others, in this room, who have done that.

P.   This seems to be on a regular basis, Antony.   I look forward to seeing you on Sunday.

If you see me, will you tell them what I look like?
Is there anything more that you would like to ask, Carole?

C.   No, I think you have covered such a lot tonight, and it will be very interesting to listen to it being played back.   I think Arthur will be ready to return to us?

I will keep him on the Earth a little longer.

C.   Oh, yes, please do.

So, shall we meet on Sunday, and again on Tuesday?   Bless you all, goodnight.

ANTONY SAYS ...
CHAPTER NINE

Good evening, friends, here we are again. Welcome to Maria.
I have been hearing about the good work that you have been
doing, whilst absent. That is good. Shall we start?

*C. Yes, Maria will start tonight, Antony. She has plenty of
questions here.*

*M. Yes, Antony, I wonder if you could tell us something about
euthanasia? What happens to the soul?*

You are asking about that one word?
I think that you already know that 'euthanasia' is the ending
of a life of a soul in a body, and converting it into a soul without
a body, making that soul take its transition, at a time decided
by those who feel they have that power. It is the same sort
of power that is used to abort an embryo, or to shoot a person.
It is just as drastic; just as final, for the soul in that body, and
they are all, at least, to be called 'questionable', and, most of the
time, to be deplored. God started that soul on its journey. He
gave it eternal life, with the power to make its own decisions,
as it moves on its path. None of those conditions are removed
by euthanasia. The soul retains all its rights and properties,
as it moves back to heaven, to go through the shock of reading
its report, computer recordings, on which will be recorded the
identity of the souls who have created that termination. That
will also be recorded on their own personal computers. They
will be the ones to face the questions, and to judge themselves,
as to whether they were right to go against God's own expressed
wish. That is what happens to the soul. It continues, as though
it had taken its transition in the normal way, if there is such a
thing as the normal way. It behaves as though it has been killed
in battle, murdered in a dark street, or in whatever way you like

to think.   It continues the eternal life that was given to it at the beginning.   It is a question of on who's conscience is that offence; because, it is an offence.   It can be a small one or a big one.   It can be likened to taking one's own life, a suicide, which is treated similarly.   In that case, the offence is caused by the soul in the body, about which you are talking.

But, euthanasia is a big word for a sad state of affairs.   There are many times, in many lives on the Earth plane, when the soul feels that life is not worth living, and uses that expression.   He says it to himself, or herself.   They can be deciding that life is not worth living because of pain, of illness, pain caused by unpleasant characters who wish them harm, and they can reach a point where they feel, or they know, that the pain is unbearable. This is where you might feel a little more compassion for the soul concerned, a little more sympathy with the suicide who is driven beyond the pale, driven past their wits' end, with pain or fear, to the point where they do something that terminates their life in that body.   With euthanasia, the decision is made by persons other than the one concerned.   He or she might have asked to have their life terminated, for the same reasons that I mentioned about the suicide.   On the other hand, they might not have made the request; the decision to end their life could have arisen from other thoughts.   It could have been decided that they are in pain and should be 'put down', like a veterinary surgeon would put an animal in pain 'down', to prevent further suffering. The decision could have been made by others, who wish that life to end, so that they gain property, valuables or whatever, just greed; that would be an appalling offence, but, it happens. Sometimes, a decision is made to commit that offence because the patient is unable to express themself.   They are what you call 'brain-dead', irreparable; who knows that?   Who decides that a patient can never come out of a coma and resume life?   That joyful occasion has happened many times.   People have come out of a coma after many months, or even years.

To go back to those committing euthanasia, they are putting themselves into the position of God, which is something that no one soul in my group would dream of doing, or would dare to do. We have too much respect for God and his will. I could go on. Would you like more?

M. Yes, because we were always told that people, who commit suicide, wander and the soul would not be accepted, until their life time on Earth would have finished.

No, no, that is imagination, imaginary thinking. The soul has taken its transition, through the action of the person it was, when in a body. That soul could be treated with extreme kindness, consideration, sympathy, empathy, by those who greet it on its arrival in heaven, those who have been watching the situation, and watching what has caused that moment of 'madness', if you like, where the decision was made, and the action taken. No, do not condemn that soul to a lower level, because of the action. The soul will go the level to which it would have gone, if it had continued to work for the rest of the lifetime on Earth. No, judgement is for the soul concerned, not for you, or for me, or any others, who are aware of the suicide. Do not judge them. Send them healing thoughts. Wish them well, because they will be in an unhappy state when they realise the mistake that they have made. Those of us, who have seen many such souls arrive, find it very easy to offer our sympathy and loving help; and they need it.

M. Is there a special way or exit for the soul when it leaves the body?

Do you mean, physically, does it leave the body through the head, or the heart, or somewhere?

M. Yes, that question often pops up.

Ah, well, there's an answer for it, and I will give you that answer.

CHAPTER NINE

The soul occupies the body, almost completely. It might not have much feeling in the toe nails, or the finger nails, but it almost completely occupies the space of that body. When it is time to go, for whatever reason, (reasons that we have mentioned), when it naturally reaches the end of its time, it goes. It is not there any longer. If you like to sit beside somebody, who is about to take their transition, and you may have done so; you are holding their hand, you feel the occasional pressure, you speak to them, but they do not answer, their hand is warm, your hand is warm. You are linked with them, spiritually; you are giving them healing and loving thoughts. You know they are there, and, if you are very, very, quick; no, before then, even, the next thing is for the heart to stop beating. You have been holding the pulse of their left wrist. You have been watching the monitor, and the pulse stops, and you think that they have gone. You didn't see them go. You are pretty sure that they have gone; and then the pulse starts again! They had not gone. They were teasing. A few seconds later, or a minute or two later, the pulse stops again, and does not restart.

And that is where, if you were very quick, watching to see whether the soul would emerge from the head, from her mouth, from the eyes, her forehead, from her chest, and you, if you were extremely quick, and watching; you would not see anything. They had gone. And, if you look up to the ceiling on the opposite corner, away from the bed, they are there, watching you. Laughing. Thinking, it was easier than I thought. And that is what they feel. It was simple. They don't know whether they came out of the left ear, or the right ear, or where. The soul was in that body, and then, suddenly, it was not there.

That soul cannot be weighed or measured. You know what we think about weighing or measuring people? So the body does not change weight. One moment it was a live body; and then it wasn't! So, I defy anybody to say where the soul exited from the body. It was a different dimension. It was there, and then it wasn't there. It may have gone inwards, not outwards. You are thinking physically, of a physical body, with something in it which has to get out.   It is not that at all.   There is something in it, which you call a soul, which, suddenly, is in a different dimension.   It is up there, in the corner, watching, wondering why on Earth you are puzzled.

Why would people make definite statements like that?

Because some of them have been in a situation, like I have described, waiting for someone to die, has said, yes, I saw the soul come out of the top of the head, it is like a wisp of steam. They have said that.   That was their imagination.   They could not see it, because it did not come out of the top of the head.   It went.   It went to a different vibration, a different frequency, a different universe, call it what you like.   People who make dogmatic statements like that could ask more, or they could make more interesting statements, they could be more constructive, more positive.   It could be that they merely wanted to appear to have seen a sight that nobody else would admit to seeing. People are motivated by all sorts of reasons, conditions.   I think that is all I can give you.

M.   That gives me great peace, on that occasion.   Ian has gone home, then?   Ian is with you, up there?

Is that a question?

M.   Yes, that was.

Which Ian are you talking about?

M.   Who passed over a few weeks back.

A lot of 'Ians' have passed over lately.   It is a very popular name.

Is it the one you were concerned with, with your friend, oh, yes, you should say that.   I can find him now.   Yes, he is making movement, the one I am looking at now; he has awakened to the situation, he is aware of it, he is welcomed by many others, which is normal, it is usual. There is no need to have any more anxiety about his soul, or any other that has passed over, recently. They are relieved of pain, stress, anxiety; for whatever reason, they feel better, even if they have been caused to go before their time, their planned time. They feel better on arrival, free of a lot of silly restrictions, a lot of wrong ideas, and they become aware of things. They become aware of spiritual values. They are especially aware of the prayers and the healing thoughts that are sent to them, which they know, they acknowledge, as they settle in. They adapt to a much happier, more pleasant, state of affairs. There is a continual process of souls taking their transition. Every second of every minute of every day, somewhere, they are doing just that. We see it. Spirit see it, through all the eyes, and links, that we have, through all the linked groups and members, linking with the groups, and the newly established ones that have been at this side for a little time. They all see it. It is a continual process. Each one is noted. Each one is recorded. And, each one reads their own recordings of their life, and decides how they can make progress in the future, on their long path ahead. Thank you.

C. Is there anything you want to ask, Phyllis?

P. Antony, you spoke about the people who have to face the consequences of their thoughts, if they help people to pass. Do the vets have to face different feelings, as well, when they have to put animals down?

It is all recorded. There is a recording of everything they do, everything you do, everything I do, everything Carole does, everything Arthur does. It is all recorded. But, you face that, when you take your transition.

So, a veterinary surgeon, is putting down an animal in pain, one that is reaching the end of its life, unable to enjoy its food, or its life; they are very clever people, and they don't do that for the pleasure of killing. Murderers, soldiers, do that. So, they do it to help the creature. If there had been no veterinary surgeon available, that creature would have crept under a bush, in a wood, somewhere, and lain there without drinking, without eating, waiting for death, which would come, and it would take its transition. It is much kinder, as it is approaching that time, for a doctor, a veterinary surgeon, to ease it out of this world, free of pain. When you look into the eyes of an animal in that position, being taken to a vet's surgery for examination, you can see it in the animal's eyes; it knows it is going to be looked after. It knows that the help is going to come from that man, or that woman, who is holding that needle. It doesn't complain. It accepts it, and goes to sleep. The most natural thing of living is dying, or taking a transition, whether it is today at five o'clock, or today at half past five; you can measure it on your clocks, but it is not of importance.

So, someone who decides to terminate their own life a day or two, or a few days, before nature would have taken its course and taken them away, they are not to be criticised. They just need the awareness of what they have done, and they will always have that awareness. They are not condemned. They are not punished for it. They need help and sympathy and healing, compassion. Those are the feelings that they should arouse. The only time where there should be consideration of punishment is where people are deliberately killed, for the wrong reasons. Right?

P. Thank you Antony. I would like to ask something for myself, if I may?

Would I be permitted to know who my guides and helpers are?

You are permitted to know, if they tell you their names. If they withhold their names, you are not permitted to know. It is their decision.

You will remember how long it was; but, that was before you came into this group. I would not give my name to Carole and Arthur all last year, because it was embarrassing. I knew that, if I told them it, they could not remember it, they could not pronounce it, so I saved them embarrassment by saying, no, I don't give my name, that is not permitted. You may call me the visitor, which they did, happily, for many months. I am still the visitor. I am still visiting you and them, but, can you pronounce my name?

P. No. my dear, I can't.

So I am glad I did not leave it. Thank you.

P. I would even like to know the nationality. I think I am aware of the nationality, but I would like Antony to confirm it

Let me tell you, there are no nations, there are no religions, in heaven, and you guides come from heaven. They dress up in their fancy costumes, the colour of their skin, the way their hair is tidied, the strange, old ways of the Indian brave, the Zulu warrior, the little Chinaman; we know them all. Carole had a little Chinaman for many, many, months, before she found out his name. She asked but did not get his name. Eventually, it was given. And he is still with her. So, they are still on speaking terms.

C. Not always.

I might ask you to explain that!

C. Right, next question. Are you ready for this?
Could you explain the work your group is doing to achieve a higher awareness of spirit? I understand, from a previous meeting, it was to do with evil?

I suppose, if you look back at my definition of 'spirit', it is all to do with fighting evil. Spirit, they call it, (or they call them), the Holy Spirit in the Church of England, the Roman Catholic Church, and others; Holy because we are part of God's plan. Some time ago, it was recorded that the Holy Spirit is there to look after the healing, and the 'newly dead', for want of a better word. Roughly, that could be a reasonable description of most of our work. Because we have these links, and, you know, I know, that each soul in a body on the Earth has almost always more than one, sometimes quite a number of guides and healers, fellow travellers, call them what you will; they spend a lot of time, a long time, years, sometimes all of a life, looking after that soul. They are the conscience. If that soul thinks, should I do this, should I do that? That is the right thing to do, but the other looks more interesting, even if it is wrong, or naughty. The guides, or conscience, are there, reading those thoughts, continually monitoring what that soul in a body is doing. It could say, yes, if you go for the naughty option, you may have a thrill, but you may regret it later. The right thing to do is to go left. If you go right, you will be left, behind; just to confuse people! They help you to weigh up the options at a crossroads, or diversion on the road, to help you to assess what is the best thing to do. And, when you have decided that, you may still do the opposite, and go the other way. But, that is your decision, and that will be logged in your little notebook. The guides will be there. They can give you their names. They can appear to you, if they wish, showing you what was their normal appearance in one of their past lives, an appearance that they enjoy, the Indian brave, the Zulu warrior, the Chinaman, the nun. It is amazing how many of them have been associated with religious organisations, nuns, monks, priests, rabbis. They appear in an easily recognisable way and dress, so that you can think, oh, there's my nun coming with me today; if you see her. But, nobody else can see her. All of them are working with you to make progress on their own path. They might put in a stint of eighty or ninety years with a soul in order to (I was going to say, move up one level), in order to make progress and improve their own awareness of spiritual values. They are on a path, as you are.   You might find, in one hundred years time, that you are a guide for one of them, who has returned to the Earth plane, returning the favour.   Or, they may have done it for you before. There is an endless variety of associations of spirits.

C.   Can I just interrupt there, a moment?
   The question that I asked is about your group, itself, I know you are linked with all the other groups, as you mentioned before, but, what are you actually trying to achieve in your group in your further awareness?

Anything that we achieve, in our group, will help the other linked groups that are with us, particularly those that are immediately around us, above us and just below us.   They are already ninety per cent aware of what we are doing, or, one hundred per cent aware of what we are doing, depending on their advancement. In answer to the question, what are we doing?   One of us, at this moment, is linking with you and your friends here, for the purpose of channelling your thoughts, your logic, in a slightly different direction; very slightly, in order to open you awareness of new aspects of spirituality.   That is a long sentence, but I can put it more simply, by saying, in my own personal case, for the time that I am working with you, which is only part of my time, I am trying to nudge you, encourage you, and lead you, a little bit further ahead on your path.   That is probably an over-simplification, but that is the purpose of the time that I am spending with you.
   Everything that I do and say is noted, recorded, and listed within our group, so all the others in the group are aware of it, and, if they can find some little way of putting a thought into my mind, putting that into Arthur's mind, and coming out in words that you can understand, to help you advance, they will do so. They are all working for you, with you, in the knowledge that, as you make progress, you will be helping others to make a little progress on their path.   As you record these words, if they are put into print, and read by others, it can help to nudge them into

a slight change in their attitudes, spiritual thought. It can help to increase their already growing awareness of spirit, but it can help them to take one more step forward. If you could get everybody in the world to read that, there would be some progress for a lot of them. That is the difficulty, to get people to read the words, and receive the message that is being continually passed out to those on the Earth plane. So, our work is all of the intention of advancing God's will to bring you all to that joyful termination at the end of eternity. Bless you.

C. Bless you for that. Arthur has a question for you, what was the origin of evil, as the creator had always been there?

That is a good question. He is already one step forward, telling me that the creator has always been there, and that is using Earth time.

Evil is negative goodness. That is the best description. The goodness was there; not at the start, because there was no start. The goodness was always there, but, if you ask, was it in every possible place, all the time, for ever, from the beginning of eternity, which is a contradiction, the answer is, no. The question has been answered; I think it was in one of the holy books, by saying that there was an angel who went astray. He was tempted and fell. He was sent out of heaven. His name eventually became 'Satan', long before my time. I have always been aware of evil, but as a negative thought rather than as a positive thought. A lack of goodness; a lack of desire to help; not, always, a desire to do harm, but the lack of desire to help can create an evil situation. As far as I am aware, there have always been these different stages of awareness, from the time when souls were first given the freedom of choice to take whatever action they wished. That was the opportunity for negativity to creep in, and, because it was contrary to the idea of light, it was called darkness. On the Earth plane, in dark corners, a lot of evil is done. I cannot give you the date when it started. I understand, from long before my time, that there was an awareness of dark and light, light being good, darkness being bad. The darkness, the negativity, created all sorts of problems, which grew, and gave opportunities for good wishes and healing thoughts to correct it. It also gave the opportunity for the darkness to try to grow, and it developed its own hatred for light. The result of that, now, as you are aware, when someone walks into a room, surrounded by light, there will be those who wish to do harm to that person, that light; they will wish to give some negativity to it, spoil it, kill it, or whatever. That is the continual process; dark versus light, light versus darkness. I have told you, many times, the light will win, but don't ask me when. There is a long way to go, yet, but there are many signs of progress in that direction. Each soul, that moves forward, on its own path, is a step towards that goal; the removal of evil. That is why you have worked, in the way you have, for so long. All of you, you know what is right, you know what is wrong, and you want to do the right thing. You are doing that, spending this time, listening to me, giving you thoughts, through this complicated system which we have. The thoughts are getting through. You, each one of you, each one here in this room, has made progress. It is good. I congratulate you all, and I wish you well. May you long continue to make progress. As you encourage your minds to open up to some of the different aspects of the expressions that you have heard, different reasoning, and different logic, you will take another step forward. And that is how it goes on, always positive attitudes, moving away from negative darkness. Does that help you?

C. Yes, thank you. Arthur will be able to hear that tomorrow, when he puts it on the disc.

M. Does soul become spirit on the rebirth of a soul? Is it a continuation of the soul: it does not stop, or does it?

A soul is spirit. A spirit is not always a soul, only when it is a spirit in a body. You call it your soul because you are in a body.

ANTONY SAYS ...

If you were in spirit, you would say that you are a spirit. A soul does not stop. The life of a spirit started when God put that spark out, and gave it the freedom of thought, the freedom of choice. He also gave it eternal life, so those two things cannot be taken from it, not by any murderer, not by a 'euthanasi-ist', or whatever they call themselves. That soul cannot be killed. Euthanasia is merely removing the soul from the body, and returning it to spirit, sending it back to spirit. The life of that soul is eternal, and the only end to that life is when it returns to the white light of the bliss of reunification with God, when it has learnt everything, when it has done everything, when it has done all that it can, it is reabsorbed into God, whatever He is. Sheer bliss! I am on the way there, but I may have another few thousand, or few million years work. We don't count it. We just count the progress. We move forward, as you will, and are doing.

C. What more can we do, Antony, to advance ourselves while we are still in the body?

That is a good, positive question. Continue on the normal lines, that I have given you, replay the discs, occasionally, and refresh your memory, but, most of the principles are on your records, now. Is this the ninth visit? It is possible that, by the time you have had your tenth visit, there will be enough there, when it is typed to present in a book form, which can help many others. Arthur has to type it all; sometimes he has to type it twice, when he is careless. But, after ten visits, we might well find that we have enough to sit back, and, if you wish, play them again, talk about them again, for further inspiration, further questions. You decide for how many more weeks you wish to have these sessions. They are of benefit to you all, now, but the benefit to others, who read the book, could multiply many, many, times. I hope that you will give that some thought.

But, how you can continue to advance? I can only say, keep an open mind, with cheerful, optimistic thought; knowing that the light will win.   Continue to send out healing, at every opportunity.   That all helps.   It helps others.

You have developed an open mind during these last few weeks, so use that opening of your mind.   New thoughts will come in, and you will say, where did I get that from?   Is that a residue from Antony?   And you will then know that you have moved up a little bit on your level!

C.   I once had an experience that you will know about.   I was in sleep state, and travelling, like we do, when we leave the body, and I was taken somewhere.   I looked upon a light, which was so bright that I could not bear to look upon it.   It was so bright; I had to turn my head away from it.   Is that how bright your light is?

Not mine.   That is the light of all spirit; the great white light of spirit, which is ahead of us all.   You have seen that.   Arthur has seen it, twice.   It is dazzling.   It is so reassuring, to know that it is there.   The tremendous brightness of it will dispel any darkness.   No dark entity can get near.   That is why you know that light will always win.   I am feeling that it is near time?

C.   Yes, it is.   Are you ready for closing now?

Yes, please.

C.   We do thank you for coming, Antony, as always, and we look forward to meeting you again, next week, all being well.

Yes, I will look forward to that.   Bless you all.

ANTONY SAYS ...
CHAPTER TEN

My greetings to you, friends. I am sorry to see the Phyllis is not with us, and I wish her well.

C. She did leave a question, which we will put to you as the evening goes on. Would you like to start, Maria?

M. Yes, Antony, I would like to know more about karma. What does karma stand for?

You give me another language. There is some Hindi and some Urdu in Arthur's vocabulary. I believe that with karma you are referring to what the English call fate? Am I right?

M. Yes.

You don't sound very happy?

M. Perhaps, I should let you talk, and then I can come back to explain it.

My explanations are limited, and the words I use are limited, to those in Arthur's vocabulary. If you agree that you would like me to talk about a fate, a destiny, which you may refer to as having some of the meaning of karma.

Each spirit, created by God, which becomes a soul in a body, a living spirit, has its own future ahead of it. Parts of it are planned. Parts of it are left open. The open parts are those where the spirit makes the decision to go one way, or another, when met with an alternative path in front. We have explained it a number of times. The spirit will have that choice; the opportunity to make a decision will not be taken away. There are those who suggest that God should rule the world, and stop all this nonsense, stop all this war, fighting, bickering, disagreement, and make life peaceful. They are suggesting that God goes against his word. His word was that each soul had the right to make its own decisions. That right also meant that the responsibility for those decisions was with that soul.

Freedom of choice. That is not destiny; that is not karma. That is where the soul can go against any planned future. Now, you are already aware of the difficulty of translating heavenly time into Earth time, and vice versa, but we will try. Each soul, apart from having a freedom of choice at decision time, also has a path. That path could be called its destiny.

It is a path which must be travelled, from beginning to end, (and you know the end, and you know the beginning), but, between those two points, certain things will, happen, whether the soul wants them to happen or not, whether it is aware of them or not, and, if it is aware, whether it wants to fight against them, or not. That, which we are talking about, is the predestined future of events which will affect that soul. I feel that we are around the fringe of your word 'karma', so you might feel like asking, what are the facts of this karma, this destiny?

The first was that the soul would become an independent spark of God's love. There is also a very great likelihood, in fact, I would say, almost one hundred per cent certainty, that that soul will find a time, on its path, when it wishes to develop, from its experience, of being a soul in a body. In other words, it will start a life of a foetus, an embryo, and a child. It may well survive childhood, and grow to have a few more years experience. So, that can be part of destiny, karma, a future, a fixed future, that that child will have a life. The sort of life it has is selected, with influence from the soul itself, the desire to have certain experiences; learn certain facts, learn certain aspects of life in a soul in a body. That can be part of its destiny. It is usual, in recording the programme for that soul, on a time scale, using heavenly time, not Earthly time, to have a starting date and a finishing date. That can easily be written in Earth time. You could say, when a child is born, it is on record when it will return home, to heaven. That is a planned date. And you also know that it is possible for that planned date to be changed by outside influence. That life in a body can be terminated by a sudden change of circumstances. It can be murdered. It can kill itself, suicide. It can go to war. But, even in those circumstances, many went to war, walked through a variety of conditions, with explosions, and rapid-firing weapons, sending projectiles close enough to touch the body of that soul, when they still survived. That happens. That is where destiny, karma, asserted itself, and yet, it is not a free spirit of its own. But, the rules were applied, and that soul survived. There are plenty of examples. The choice of occupation, work; the use and development of talents, artistic talents, creative talents, gifts from God, can be considered karma. Each one soul, with an independent life, and ability in decision making, has some talent from God. Opportunities will be placed in front of it, to aim for its destiny, to become an athlete, sportsman, an artist, an architect, a leader of men; all the different talents are available to different people, different souls. They, then, apply their own desire, to make a decision, and then either go ahead to develop that talent, or they belittle it, especially when they are told that it is God-given. They belittle it, ignore it, and let it fade. That is wasted talent. There are plenty of opportunities for studying that aspect. Then there is the possibility that that soul has given way to negativity, sent out unkind thoughts, done unkind deeds, and applied unkind pressures, on another soul to hurt them, for various reasons. Jealousy, greed, ego, come back again and again; or it can be simply evil, darkness, dark entities affecting the soul in that body and encouraging hurt to others, the creation of more evil, more pain, misery, death, sudden unexpected unpleasantness. That can be having an affect on karma, as you call it, destiny.

No one can continually send out evil without there being repercussions, natural repercussions and unnatural ones. There are those who believe that a debt is created by sending out evil thoughts, unkind wishes; that a debt is created to the one who suffers. It could be said that the one owes something to the other. They use the expression, working off a karmic debt. These are all different ways of saying that there are repercussions from sending out evil thoughts, doing evil things. There are ways of the world, ways of the heavens, to bring to the mind of evil-doers, that they are wrong, and that they have to accept the responsibilities for their actions. That is one of the reasons why the recording of all their moments, thoughts, words deeds, in their life, are shown to them when they return home. They become aware of owing a debt, a kindness to repay an unkindness. We could go on all night, talking about those.

M. I have always understood that, if a life is cut short, by accident, or murder, the soul concerned must come back here and be reborn, in order to complete the span of life on the Earth plane that had been in the original plan. You say the plan can be altered by circumstances?

Did that soul, which was parted from the body by an accident or disaster, not come back; but to where? That soul exists. That soul cannot be deleted. The soul exists, it has eternal life.

M. Yes, that I do understand. No, that soul was returned home by an accident. Does it come back here to complete the remainder of the planned life here, its destiny?

The destiny was to have a life over a period, planned before it started that life. Then I said that, it can happen, that there is a murder, killing by accident, in action in the army, the navy, the air force, or even suicide can alter that plan. That plan was the destiny. The alteration of the time scale happened because of some force, good, bad, or evil. Some force was brought to bear, and it changed the arrangement. That is why it is sad, when the soul in the body makes the decision to terminate itself with suicide. That is sad, and sometimes bad, but it is always sad. When that termination is caused by another party, that is bad. Killing, murder; if it is different from what was planned, it is bad. That can create an imbalance in the destiny, the karma, of that soul, if the termination comes before the planned date. We had a question, last week, where the doctors took pity on an old dying soul, what was the word? Euthanasia, they took pity, and they felt that they were doing the right thing, to relieve the pain and the anxiety, by giving treatment that had the possibility, and in some cases the certainty, of terminating that life on Earth, earlier than was expected. He may have been a few hours, a few days, or a few weeks early. You have to balance that improper procedure, with the good intentions, however warped they may or may not have been, the good intentions of those causing that speedier transition. Each case is different. Each case is assessed separately. Each one of those involved will face that when they report for duty with their own little computer records. There is no rule to say, this will happen to them, other than the fact that they will have to look at a replay of the incident, and judge themselves. They will judge themselves, anyway. They all do. So, the judgement is ahead of them, but it is their own personal judgement. They cannot adjust the balance before they make the judgement; they are given the facts, because the facts are within them. So, if you are looking for more about destiny, or karma, or a planned future, or whatever you like to call it, you come back to the fact that each soul has its own destiny, makes its own judgements, decides what the future holds, what form of training, development, whether they can forgive themselves or not. That is the judgement. Does that help you?

M.   Er, yes.

Sounds doubtful?

M.   Perhaps, another time. The other one is rebirth, ongoing, is each soul privileged to come back here, to reach its destiny, or another pathway, with a rebirth?

A rebirth is not guaranteed. One time rebirth did not occur.

CHAPTER TEN

We have talked about it. You have read about it. It was found that one life on the Earth plane lasted anything from a few minutes, to about thirty years, but still not long enough to make any great progress on the path. You know that we are always experimenting. You have heard that expression before? We have experimented with Arthur, with his book. We have experimented with him, using his vocabulary, for me to talk to you, whilst I am thinking in something entirely different, and communicating with you. These are experiments.

Experiments were carried out, after a period of time, rest, rehabilitation, extra training, in heaven, when a returned soul realised how little progress it had made on the Earth plane and asked for permission, asked for the ability, to come back and have a second time here. That was an experiment. And, it was tried, with a few, and it worked. Even when they came back, the second time, with a clean memory, cleared of any history of a previous life on Earth; they came back, started again, and I have always believed there is a very fine trace of previous experience on Earth, for those who come back a second time. It comes with such feelings as, I have been here before, I have seen this mountain before, I have seen this valley before, whether it is or not difficult to prove, but, I feel convinced that those, coming a second time, have a slight advantage, they make a little more progress. They use their time a little more wisely. They are more receptive to spiritual thoughts. They are more creative. They have made that weapon before. They have painted that picture before. They have done something like that before. They don't know that, but it sometimes looks as though they had that ability carried forward. And it is good that they should make further progress. That is the whole desire of the system.

After a period of time, they feel the desire to have a third life, and further progress was made. Things developed. They had an increased awareness of possibilities. This was developed on and on, through the centuries, through the millions of years. We now have souls who have had ten, twenty, or more, lives in the Earth plane; and they can be regressed. They can have an awareness of those previous lives, so they know they have had previous lives. They know they have lived in different parts of the world. They recognise the places. And then, we come to the point where it is said, that trouble-maker is a new soul, but that other one over there, the wise man, he is an old soul. He has been here a long time; he has been here many times. He is more advanced; and that is a possible explanation for that situation.

C. Thank you. Moving on, Antony, Arthur wanted me to ask you this question. We seem to have recorded so many questions, and your answers, that there is sufficient material for a book. Are there any more questions and answers that you would have liked to be included?

First of all, he feels ready to complete his typing work and publish these previous records in book form? That would be a very good idea, from my point of view, in that the time I have spent with you, and with Phyllis, this small group, has then been productive, and the information could be helpful to anyone, who has a spiritual nature, who wishes to read it. It could have benefit. It could be a good thing.

So, is he telling me that, if I don't get all the questions that I want, they are going to be omitted? Or, is he saying that, if I don't get all the questions I want to be asked and answered, I will keep you here, week after week, until you do your homework?

C. I don't think so. I think you are joking with us.
Is there anything that you would have liked to have covered, or talked about, that we have not thought of, that would be instructive to others?

I am looking at the range of knowledge that we have covered, from, what you might have called, the lower levels, up to six or seven. We are on the fringe of eight, with one or two of the questions, which have been good. Questions and answers have indicated that you are opening your minds and looking well ahead, thinking well ahead and wanting help to move well ahead. That is, by far, a wide enough range of ability, a scope of ability. I would not suggest questions, where the answers would not be understood. It would not be helpful. So, looking back on the questions that you have asked, these will be put down in a list of contents, will they not, indicating which questions are asked in each chapter?

I have a question for each of you, now, a simple one. You have formed this group, which has made excellent progress, for the time and effort applied, and for the small numbers of you involved. You have all made excellent progress. Have you thought of a name for yourselves, for your group?

C.   No, I haven't.   It didn't occur to me.

One of the first questions that I was asked was, am I a member of the White Brotherhood Group?

C.   Well, I know what group I belong to.

Yes, but that is a spiritual group, a part of spirit, the linked spiritual group that we have discussed. Yes, I am part of that group, you are part of it, we all are. We are all linked. But, your little group of four souls, yes, one, two, three, four, I have got that right. My arithmetic has not slipped too much. That small group; you should think of yourselves as having worked together, moved forward together, and you all have; you should think of yourselves with a name. Let me think of one for you. You could call it, (I was thinking of one for you), you could call it the AMPAC Group, but that doesn't mean anything. IMPAC. The Impac Group. I am in it, M for Maria is in it, P for Phyllis is in it, A for Arthur is in it, and C for Carole is in it. There is only one thing missing.

C.   What about the T?
Tea.   You have that when you finish!   So, you then make

ANTONY SAYS ...

IMPACT!

It is a thought.

I do not think that there are any deep questions that we need to inject into the system this evening, in order to have it included in the book. We can see how this works; see whether there is a possible distribution of these books, and how big that distribution can be.

C.   I think that it will be more helpful, as we go round the churches this year, to hand one of these books to each church. I think that would be helpful, for those speaking.

We could include, somewhere in the glossary, or whatever they call it, a suggestion that, those who wish, and those who enjoyed the question and answer session, whether in the Impact group or not; whether they had seen the questions and answers in the book, and enjoyed the system, and would like to ask questions themselves, we can show them how to do it. We can tell them how to do it. They can form their own little group, in their own locality. They can invite me. One of my group will certainly be willing, ready, available, to come and give them the answers to their questions, in the same way that I am doing it now. So, that is a good suggestion. Thank you, we will incorporate that.

C.   Moving on from there, there is a question here from Phyllis, that I have left to the end.   When you were on the Earth plane, were there any different animals then?

What made her think that I had been on the Earth plane, other than visiting, like this?

C.   Reading the book, I would think. I can't answer that, because she is not here.

She knows that I am getting quite old. She knows I was here with Ywancontin, five million years ago; just a moment in time.

There were different animals then. She read about them in the book; the sabre-toothed tiger, the big cats, a whole variety of big, furry, creatures, with huge appetites; who could run faster than the hominids, who could catch them quicker, and kill them before they could use their weapons, in the early days. But, the hominids survived and grew into mankind, whereas the big cats shrank and became little pussy cats. At times, they can be vicious, as you know.

C. Yes, we have one here.

There we are. Is she thinking of the dinosaurs?

C. I think she is thinking of the prehistoric animals.

These animals, the cats, are prehistoric; and the alligators, the forerunners of the crocodiles. They used to love to lie in the shallows, waiting for other creatures coming to drink the water, and then they would have a meal. Great fun! For the crocodile!

Yes. The answer is yes. There were many, many, other animals, but I do not go back to the dinosaurs, as I was elsewhere at that time.

C. We won't go into that, as I know you don't want to. Have you anything else you want to ask, Maria?

M. Yes, it has to do with my healing. Why is it that, from where I am sitting, and looking at people, I get the impression that some of the people go forward quicker than others. Do some people get more support from above than others, or is it due to the individual?

That is a good question. We are back at the old business of measuring, aren't we? More support? How do you measure support?

ANTONY SAYS ...

Each soul has the same right to make its own decisions. Each soul has eternal life. So, those two things, the two important things, are the same for everyone. Live for ever, and decide what to do, for ever. We were talking, last week, about people making progress faster than others. There is a tendency for a soul to be static for a time, resting, and then they can move forward. Over a long period of time, that is progress. There are others, who go on a training course with an advanced spirit, and they have week after week of questions and answers, from which they learn. They learn to open their minds, look forward, look higher, look ahead, seeking a different light, having a greater awareness, and suddenly they realise that they know a little more. They are looking at things differently, and one or two of us in this room are aware of that, are we not? They make more progress, with a few weeks like that, than some people make in a few lifetimes! Believe me, a few lifetimes' progress could have been made by you individuals here now. If you continue to think, on the lines on which you have been trained to think, understanding that you can see that differently, that you can see this better, you know what to do under those circumstances better, you are able to help other people more, more frequently, more deeply. You know that you have made progress, not just a little bit that one might make in a lifetime. You could have made progress, when you apply all these thoughts, for the rest of your time, your eyes opened wider, your ears opened wider, your computer going at top speed recording all the thoughts that you are having. You know that you have made more progress than you did in the last three lives. That is very good, is it not? Be proud of it. Mark it down. Do not press the delete button. Keep it. Keep the record.

Now, what was your question?

M. Yes, should I have said, some are more recognised than others, who have not got the ability to put themselves forward? Do you mean, are there some students of spiritual life, who are favoured by the instructors, the school teacher types, who, are not only favoured but who are nudged, at the right time, in the right direction, encouraged to take that step forward; and others not being given that same encouragement? That sort of thinking could be one way of looking at spiritual instruction, but it is not quite open, not quite an honest assessment of what is happening. Each soul, in a body, is recognised by God, as one of his. He does not have favourites, like a school teacher might have. He has given to that soul exactly what he has given to each soul before, and which will be given to each soul afterwards, as new souls are created and started on their way. Some learn slowly; some learn less slowly. Believe me, they all learn very, very, slowly, indeed. You do. I do. That is why it takes a long time to make progress. That is why I am here, because it is our group wish to help things to move forward, at a rate that will ensure the destruction of darkness. We are not speeding up because we are in fear of darkness. We are trying to increase the speed a little for the sheer joy of being right; knowing it is right, knowing it is good. We, in our group, have moved forward slowly but surely. Everything that you do, as a result of our visit to you; everyone who reads this book, which is yet to be typed and finished and published; everyone who reads the book will know a little more, and make a little more progress than they may have made, standing still, sitting down, waiting for heaven to open up and expect them. It is all part of the plan, part of the progress. Does that help you?

M. Yes, recognition on this Earth plane does not matter.

There is no connection between those in high positions on the Earth plane, and the state of awareness that they have, or will have, when they return home. You have only to read your bible to find things like that. There is reference to rich men and poor men; it is easier for a camel to go through the eye of a needle, than for a rich man to reach heaven. That is a pretty strong statement, and we have had some rich men who have come to heaven. They all come to heaven. It is a question of whereabouts in heaven they go. And, they have problems. Those who worship money, and hurt others, and give people misery and pain, in order to create more wealth for themselves, they have fascinating days, contemplating their computer records. They realise then, I have not brought it with me! They would not let me bring it with me! All that gold! What a shame!

No, there is no connection at all. Some of the biggest rogues are in the highest places, where they can do the most damage. You get plenty of publicity about dictators and politicians, and kings and queens. Some of them have an awful time, facing the actual future; some of them manage. But, do not judge them. As we said last week, assess their attitudes, assess their failings. This is where making progress helps you to assess other people's strengths and weaknesses, without judging them. A harsh word, from an unpleasant contact, can sometimes bring a strong reaction, but, all that is needed is comfort, forgiveness, (if they have been unpleasant), and healing.

C. Would you like to close now, Antony?

If you feel it is time? Then, we will give Arthur a few weeks to get this book through the typing, the editing, I know what he has got to do to get this book prepared, and to find a printer, a publisher. I will be linking with him regularly, as I do, almost every day. So, I will still be in touch. I will still be available, and I will do what I can to help you with that problem that you raised. I wish you well for the future. Bless you all.

A MESSAGE TO ALL OUR READERS

It is hoped that you have enjoyed, and been surprised by, reading this book.
Did you have any of the following thoughts?:-
  I never knew that.
  I always understood differently.
  That explains why it happened to me.
  I would have liked to ask him a further question.
  I feel better for knowing that.
  I would like to have been there when he came through.

Well, you can ask for more.
   It is a fact that spirit is seeking more and closer contact with those 'in bodies', those on the Earth plane. The sole purpose is to help to improve the spiritual awareness of all of you who are on your path forward.
   There is a growing number of groups, similar to the Impact group, who meet regularly, over a period of time, and record the discussions with the intention of publishing the knowledge gained to help others. The amount of unpublished information is endless, so, there is always more to learn!
   If you would like to be part of such a group may I give you a few guide-lines to help you to form your own group:-

1. Suggest to a few of your friends that you have been impressed with this book and ask if they would like to read it and to consider making and reinforcing your own link with spirit. Four or five members would be suitable, at the start.

2. At the first meeting, the chairman could open with a request for all mobile and land line telephones to be disconnected, followed by a prayer for protection and advice. If you have a digital voice recorder it will simplify the creation of a permanent record, but please ensure that the battery is new and that it is placed on a cushion or book to ensure that it does not vibrate.

ANTONY SAYS ...

3. Soon after the start of a silence, spirit will speak through one of the members. It could be the most fluent speaker present. You will understand, from reading this book, that the communication with spirit has certain limitations. The link can only use the vocabulary and memory of the selected speaker. This enables a rapid flow of instant conversation with any one of the other members present. Regular practice will improve the speed of contact and the fluency of each session.

4. We wish to help you. All you need is the will, and a little faith!

Bless you all in your endeavours.

Antony (Ywahuntae)

Whenever Arthur Freer tried to imagine the progress of the human race, from early times, he was aware that it had survived mainly because of the two strong traits of self preservation and the ability to mate at any time of day or night.

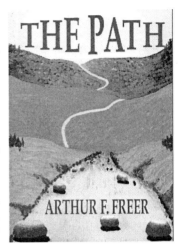

In THE PATH, he takes the reader on a journey, through the past 5 million years, from the time when the early hominids began to move out of the forests in order to explore the unknown. He lives with these primitive creatures, as their brains develop and their enquiring minds ask the questions that we still hear today. What is it all about? Why do we have to suffer? What happens after death?

This is the story of man's migratory life caused by curiosity and need. We share time with him in order to learn to control fire, to observe the horror of the great Flood, and the introduction of a range of weapons, starting with the hand-held stone, the spear and the bow and arrow. We begin to understand the effect that the use of rudimentary language had on the existing telepathic form of communication, the possible explanation of race memories of the disappearing tribes of the Trolls and the Yeti.

You may travel with the more spiritual Bear tribe, as they wend their way from southern Asia to the point where they take the opportunity to cross the Bering Straits, to enter the New World of the Americas.

The capture and control of the horse enabled man to spread his aggressive passions faster and further. The uncontrolled rapid growth in the size of the population leads to the present time, with the pollution of the land, the sea and the air.

Is there sufficient time for mankind to learn to respect this finite planet, and to survive`?

An overview of the entire period of 5 million years is given through the minutes of the ethereal committee directed to monitor our progress. They had noted that the early introduction of compassion to one female hominid had been spreading throughout a large percentage of the population. Is that our only hope for survival?

ANTONY SAYS ...

Review copies will be sent in return for an official letter giving the name of the reviewer and the likely date for the publication of the review.

Further copies of this book and copies of *The Path* can be ordered from the author.
Please send your cheque to.-

Arthur F Freer   Telephone 01733 347874
1 Westbrook Park Close
Woodston
Peterborough
PE2 9JQ

Antony Says . . .   £5.00

The Path   £5.00

Please add for post and packing: in the U K £1.00 per book
in the E U £2.00 per book
elsewhere £4.00 per book

CDs for each chapter of *Antony Says* . . . are available at £5 post paid. It is a joy to hear them.